2004

ENGAGING MINDS

Motivation and Learning in America's Schools

David A. Goslin

ScarecrowEducation
Lanham, Maryland, and Oxford
2003

A SCARECROWEDUCATION BOOK

Published in the United States of America
by ScarecrowEducation, Inc.
An Imprint of The Rowman & Littlefield Publishing Group
4501 Forbes Boulevard, Suite 200, Lanham, Maryland 20706
www.scaroweducation.com

PO Box 317, Oxford, OX2 9RU, UK

British Library Cataloguing in Publication Information Available

Library of Congress Cataloging-in-Publication Data
Goslin, David A.
Engaging minds : motivation and learning in America's schools / David
A. Goslin.
    p. cm.
    "A ScarecrowEducation book."
    Includes bibliographical references (p.   ) and index
    ISBN 0-8108-4713-2 (pbk. : alk. paper)
    1. Motivation in education—United States. 2. Learning. I. Title.
LB1065 .G67 2003
370.15'4—dc21

                                                2002154845

CONTENTS

PREFACE

This book has its origin in three interrelated questions:

- Why has it proven to be so difficult to improve America's schools?
- Why don't most students work very hard, most of the time, in school?
- When students do learn, what causes them to become engaged in learning?

As a sociologist, social psychologist, and participant in American education, as well as a parent, these questions have been a constant source of both inspiration and frustration for me over the four decades of my career. They have been an inspiration because together they seem to me to lie at the heart of the educational process. They are a source of frustration because the answers to them have proven to be elusive, not only to me but seemingly to everyone involved with education in this country.

All of the evidence that exists about what makes students and schools successful, from the scientific to the anecdotal, points to student motivation and engagement in the learning process as crucial variables. Examples of successful teachers like Jaime Escalante, who taught calculus to his inner-city students in Los Angeles, and successful schools like

Deborah Meier's Central Park East Secondary School in New York City, along with data demonstrating the importance of parental involvement in and support for their children's learning, all support the conclusion that high expectations for performance, coupled with a powerfully nurturing support system, make a real difference in learning. Simply put, if students believe they can learn and are persuaded to exert the necessary effort, they will succeed.

The purpose of this book is to examine the many things that affect student engagement in learning and to explore the implications of the results of this examination for educational policy and practice. Overall, my objective is to identify ways of increasing the frequency and duration of occasions on which more young people are engaged in acquiring important intellectual skills.

In setting forth this goal, I must admit at the outset to making at least one very important assumption: that acquiring intellectual (academic) skills is a desirable goal for most, if not all, children in this society. Although disagreements may exist about how much of what kinds of specific skills we should expect children to learn, there can be little debate about the relevance of a range of academic skills for participation in American society and the world at large in the twenty-first century. I take as a given, therefore, that increasing the motivation and engagement of the nation's young people in learning in school is a worthwhile goal.

At the same time, every parent recognizes that academic skills are not the only skills that are important for children to learn in order to be happy and successful in their lives. Parents, along with schools, are properly concerned about broader aspects of children's development, including character, physical skills, and the abilities necessary to deal with people. As one child development expert noted, the home-based educational policy of the family deals with all of these things, sometimes sacrificing a focus on academic achievement to ensure that children have an opportunity to acquire other skills and experiences that are regarded as equally important. Striking an appropriate balance among often competing goals for the nation's young people, therefore, is a central theme of this book.

This book is written primarily for an audience of professionals and others concerned about improving the quality of elementary and secondary schools in the United States, including educators, school board members, faculty of schools of education and other teacher-training institutions, legislators and other government officials concerned with education, and, of course, parents. While it draws extensively on behavioral and social science theory and research, it is not primarily an academic treatise and no claim is made here that I have reviewed all of the relevant scientific literature, which in the fields of learning and motivation alone is voluminous. In addition to the relevant research literature, I am indebted to many recent observers of American education for their insights into what makes schools tick.

The book begins by introducing the concept of engagement in learning and then poses the question of why our school system is so impervious to improvement. The answer seems to be that only a small proportion of the nation's students—perhaps as few as 20 or 25 percent—are engaged in learning most of the time. In chapter 2, I explore in greater depth what is meant by engagement in learning and outline the many things that can influence a learner's motivation to engage in learning, both initially and over time. The initial focus of the chapter is on what it takes to "start the engine" in the first place; namely, to get the learner engaged in the learning process. Next, factors that help to sustain the learner's engagement are examined, including what can be done to make learning easier. Following this overview, a conceptual framework for organizing the factors that can influence student motivation and engagement in learning is presented. This framework puts these influences into four major categories: physiological, psychological, task-related/educational, and social/cultural. The rest of the book is devoted to a detailed examination of these influences.

The third chapter considers the central issue of the extent to which one believes learning is due to ability versus effort on the part of the learner and the implications of these beliefs for the motivation and engagement of students. This discussion draws on the results of research on educational systems in other countries, especially Japan and China, which contrast sharply with American views and resulting practices. Chapter 4 takes up the role of rewards in learning and how effort is rewarded in American schools. Rewards (and the threat of punishment) play a central part in most theories of motivation, but despite almost a century of relevant research, there is still a great deal of confusion about what makes something rewarding and the conditions under which different kinds of rewards can affect motivation and learning. One of the major insights emerging from this discussion is the relative scarcity of rewards available for effort in many, if not all, of America's schools.

Chapter 5 deals with how learning is organized in America's schools and starts from the premise that effort invested by learners is a scare commodity that the nation can ill afford to waste. This chapter focuses on what can be done to increase the efficiency of learning processes to maximize returns on this investment. An important observation resulting from this discussion is that enormous inefficiencies are associated with America's almost pathological resistance to any and all efforts to standardize curricula and teaching methods.

In chapter 6, I turn to social and cultural influences on academic motivation and, in particular, to the questions of how much our society values hard work, perseverance, and self-discipline and how society's values are transmitted to young people. This analysis begins with the role of parents in inculcating and reinforcing these essential values and then turns to the crucial part played by role models outside the family, as well as institutional structures that support both families and children in their pursuit of academic goals. An important theme revolves around the implications of changes that have occurred over the last several decades in American society that have weakened these socializing influences and what might be done to strengthen them.

Chapter 7 takes up the matter of competition for the energies and effort of the nation's young people. It is clear that academic objectives must compete with a wide range of other goals that most parents have for their children in this society, including sports and the acquisition of social skills. While acknowledging both the importance and legitimacy of these competing goals, this chapter raises and attempts to answer the question of whether it is possible to strike a better balance between academic achievement and other goals for many young people.

Finally, in chapter 8, I summarize the main themes of the preceding chapters and describe in more detail the implications of these observations for policy and practice in American education, as well as for the society at large. Schools and what happens in them constitute part of the solution to the problem of increasing student engagement in learning. They may not be the most important part of the solution, however.

Helping children attain the goals set by society almost certainly will require changes on the part of everyone in the society, however modest
these changes might be.

Like every author, I am indebted to many people for their contributions to this project. In particular, George Bohrnstedt, Elizabeth Reis-
ner, Becky Smerdon, George Wheaton, Sheldon White, and Alexandra
Wigdor read versions of this manuscript and provided many useful
comments and, at least as important, encouragement. As the book
points out, encouragement is often essential for sustaining one's motivation, and I am deeply grateful for their efforts. In addition to sub-
stantive comments and suggestions, Donald Lamm contributed invalu-
able advice on how to navigate the world of publishers. I am
particularly indebted to my former colleague Eugenia Grohman for her
extremely insightful editorial and organizational suggestions. I am also
grateful to the American Institutes for Research for providing me with
an office and to Blanchie Kelley for her assistance during the last year.
Finally, my special thanks go to my wife, Nancy McGirr, without whose
constant love, support, encouragement, and faith, this book could not
have been completed.

❶

INTRODUCTION

One of the intriguing paradoxes of education in the United States is that many people believe that the nation's schools are badly in need of reform, yet most people report that they are satisfied with the schools their children attend. Another is that nearly everyone acknowledges the importance of academic achievement for success in life, yet many Americans remain deeply ambivalent about how much time and effort their children should spend on schoolwork rather than sports, work, and other activities.

American ambivalence about the amount of effort children should devote to academic achievement contributes to the fact that during much of the time most students spend in school, they are less than fully engaged in learning academic skills. It also helps to explain why the nation has made so little progress in improving education despite nearly three decades of intense effort. The importance our society attaches to academic achievement, moreover, is only one of many factors that have an influence on student motivation and engagement in learning. In addition to social and cultural values associated with academic achievement, student motivation and engagement in learning are affected by a host of other variables, both individual and organizational. To the extent that academic achievement depends on student engagement in the

learning process, it should come as no surprise that improving the performance of America's schools has proven to be so difficult. An explicit
focus on the factors that affect student engagement in learning, however, has the potential to significantly increase the engagement of many
students in acquiring academic skills.

Everyone knows what it feels like to be engaged in learning something. Most people can remember the excitement and concentration invested in learning to ride a bicycle for the first time, as well as the thrill
of success. Many of us can remember hours spent in front of a piano,
practicing scales and learning to translate notes on a page into, hope-
fully, melodies. Nearly all of us can recall page after page of long divi-
sion and multiplication problems, and memorizing important dates in
history or conjugations of verbs in a foreign language. Everyone has experienced the feeling of being engaged in learning in many different
settings and contexts: talking with parents, siblings, or peers; sitting in
front of a computer or even a television screen; on a basketball or tennis court; reading a book or studying for a test; practicing a musical instrument; and, of course, in school classrooms. On some of these occasions, this has involved working with another person—a teacher,
mentor, friend, or parent. On others, we have been alone: studying a
textbook, practicing a sport or musical instrument, figuring out how to
do something on a computer, or learning how to hang wallpaper or re-
pair a piece of machinery. Whatever the learning task, however, we can
recall the psychological investment and effort—sometimes a great deal
of effort—that was required on our part, expended over a considerable
period of time.

We also remember vividly the feelings of satisfaction that came with
the realization that we had acquired a new skill or learned something we
didn't know before. Often, we became aware of our new capabilities
gradually, as they were acquired. In other cases, learning seemed to happen instantaneously, in a flash of insight or the sudden realization that
we could do something we couldn't do before. In many instances, it took
a great deal of encouragement and praise to sustain our engagement; in
others, we found that the process of learning itself was sufficient to keep
us engaged.

Most of us also can remember instances in which our engagement
in learning did not turn out so well. On some occasions, we found the

learning task to be too difficult or tedious to sustain our interest, so we disengaged, admitting failure or claiming that we weren't really interested in acquiring that knowledge or skill in the first place. Many of us can recall experiences in which our engagement in learning turned out to be very unpleasant, as was often the case in my eighth-grade Spanish class. Whatever promise I might have had as a student of foreign languages was seriously impaired by the humiliation regularly inflicted upon me by one of only two teachers in elementary and secondary school whose names I can still remember. Fortunately for me, such negative experiences were unusual, but for many of us they are all too common.

In addition to the powerful positive rewards (and punishments) associated with learning something new, these experiences of being seriously engaged in learning something stand out in everyone's mind because, for most people, *they are relatively rare*. Much of most people's time is spent involved in the routine activities of daily living, doing things that they already know how to do. Of course, everyone learns things every day talking with others, reading a newspaper or magazine, or watching television or a film. But making and sustaining the major psychological investment that is necessary to learn something difficult is not something most people do regularly. Even the vast majority of those members of society whose main preoccupation is supposed to be with learning—students in our elementary and secondary schools, colleges, and universities—spend a relatively small proportion of their time on a daily basis seriously engaged in acquiring academic skills.

Everyone also knows from experience, as well as the observation of others, that there is a great deal of variation in the energy and effort that different learners bring to different learning tasks at different times. In some instances, a person works very hard over time at acquiring new knowledge or learning a particular skill; in others, his or her attention wanders and he or she loses interest quickly. Most people also are aware that many factors influence the amount of energy they are willing to expend on any learning task, at any given time, and for how long they are prepared to sustain their engagement in the task. These factors include their physiological state, interest in the learning task, confidence in their ability to accomplish the task, goals they may have set for themselves, rewards they expect to receive, and specific characteristics of the learning task, including its difficulty. Finally, they recognize that the more energy they are prepared to invest in the learning task, the more they are likely to learn.

The central thesis of this book is very simple: *Increasing the engagement of students in learning is the key to increasing academic achievement and therefore the productivity of the U.S. educational system.* Surprisingly, there have been relatively few attempts to explicitly consider the things that affect students' engagement in the learning process and, more important, what might be done to increase engagement and motivation in learning. This is especially so in light of the evidence that a significant proportion of elementary and secondary school students are only minimally engaged in learning in America's schools. The experience of the last two decades provides ample evidence in support of this proposition.

TWO DECADES OF EFFORTS TO REFORM OUR SCHOOLS

Almost twenty years ago, the National Commission on Excellence in Education issued its landmark report, *A Nation at Risk* (1983), setting off what has become without doubt the most intense period of school reform in the nation's history. Concern about the performance of America's schools had been increasing since the mid-1970s, but it was the National Commission's report in 1983 that, as the editors of *Education Week* put it a decade later, "shocked the nation with its grim assessment of student achievement, its martial metaphors, and its dire warning of 'a rising tide of mediocrity'" (*From Risk to Renewal* 1993).

> Our nation is at risk. Our once unchallenged preeminence in commerce, industry, science and technological innovation is being overtaken by competitors throughout the world. While we can take justifiable pride in what our schools and colleges have historically accomplished and contributed to the United States and the well-being of its people, the educational foundations of our society are presently being eroded by a rising tide of mediocrity that threatens our very future as a nation and a people. . . . If an unfriendly foreign power had attempted to impose on America the

mediocre educational performance that exists today, we might well have viewed it as an act of war. . . . Our society and its educational institutions seem to have lost sight of the basic purpose of schooling, and of the high expectations and disciplined effort needed to attain them. (National Commission 1983)

The report "summoned policymakers, citizens, parents, teachers, and students to action, proclaiming that learning is 'the indispensable investment' for success in an information age" (*From Risk to Renewal* 1993). This report and the succession of reports, analyses, and critiques of our schools that followed led to literally hundreds of major public and private initiatives aimed at improving our schools. These initiatives included two national education summits attended by the nation's business leaders, governors, and the president; establishment of two sets of national education goals (for 2000 and, more recently, 2010); creation of the National Educational Goals Panel to monitor progress toward achievement of these goals; and passage of a plethora of legislation at both the state and national levels designed to stimulate improvement of our schools. What have been the results of all this effort?

Despite more than two decades of hand wringing, debate, hard work by educators and politicians, and substantial investment in a myriad of school reform initiatives, it is difficult to detect significant changes in any standardized outcome measures of school performance. Since the early 1970s, average scores of nine-, thirteen-, and seventeen-year-olds on National Assessment of Educational Progress (NAEP) tests of achievement in reading, mathematics, and science have not changed in any important way, although mathematics scores of children in all three age groups increased slightly over the period (U.S. Department of Education 2001). Average scores on the Scholastic Aptitude Test (SAT) have fluctuated somewhat, but also have remained essentially unchanged over this thirty-year period (College Board 2002). During this period, average scores of black students on both the NAEP and SAT have increased, thus narrowing the gap between white and black students somewhat, but a very significant gap in average performance remains (U.S. Department of Education 2001; College Board 2002). In a succession of studies comparing the performance of U.S. students in reading, mathematics, and science with those of other developed nations, U.S. students' scores remain near the average scores of all countries participating in the studies and have not changed significantly in the last seven years. On average, our students still perform well below the level of students in a number of other countries on these tests (see, for example, Organization for Economic Cooperation and Development 2000).[1]

THE PARADOXES OF AMERICAN EDUCATION

The picture that emerges from all of these statistics is of an education system that, overall, is remarkably resistant to change. Paradoxically, it also seems to be a system that is in far less danger of imminent collapse than the pronouncements of the National Commission on Excellence in Education would have suggested. The question that Iris Rotberg asked in 1991 seems especially pertinent today (Tanner 1993): "How is it possible that both science and math education are so poor when the U.S. continues to maintain overwhelming dominance over other advanced nations in scientific productivity?" In that same article, Tanner goes on to assert that

> Without a basically sound education system, the U.S. could not dominate the world in scientific productivity, as reflected in our international scientific awards, publications and patents and in our ability to attract the best students from the rest of the world to our universities, where our own students have no difficulty competing with the best and the brightest of other nations. Since midcentury, Americans have won more Nobel Prizes than all other nations of the world combined. (Tanner 1993, 296)

Many of the changes in society that the National Commission on Excellence in Education predicted in 1983 would take place have in fact occurred, and at a faster pace than foreseen by the commission. The pace of technological change has outstripped many of the projections of two decades ago. What is remarkable is that the U.S. economy has not collapsed; indeed, it continues to lead the world. Somehow, the nation's schools are producing a labor force that is able to keep up with the demands of the new global economy even though they are essentially the same schools that the National Commission found so wanting in 1983. What are Americans to make of this fact, along with several other apparent contradictions that confound policymakers and the public alike?

- Despite widespread agreement among policymakers and many members of the public that schools are not performing as well as they should, the majority of parents report that they are very satisfied with their children's schools, their children's teachers, their schools' academic standards, and their schools' order and discipline (U.S. Department of Education 2001).
- Despite evidence that a very significant proportion of students are performing poorly on standards-based measures of achievement, a large percentage of mothers of elementary school students report being very satisfied with both their children's and schools' performance (Stevenson and Stigler 1992).
- Despite evidence showing clearly that level of education is the most important determinant of future earnings and, ultimately, success in life, "getting good grades" ranks third (behind being a good athlete and planning to attend college) among characteristics regarded by high school students as being greatly important for having status in high school (U.S. Department of Education 2001). In a 1996 survey conducted by the National Association of Secondary School Principals, youth expressed far more positive attitudes toward friends, sports, and social activities than toward classes and learning.

EXPLORING THE CONTRADICTIONS

The explanation for the foregoing apparent contradictions lies in the fact that the American educational system is not in reality a single system that serves all students in the same way. Nor do all students relate to their schools in the same way. Schools in this country have always served a relatively small portion—perhaps 25 percent—of the population extremely well. For the most affluent, able, and highly engaged students, the American education system is clearly on a par with any educational system in the world and there is evidence that it is getting better all the time. The best students in the most affluent schools across the country encounter more rigorous curricula, more opportunities to take advanced placement courses, and more opportunities for special educational experiences, from science and mathematics competitions to college instruction. The best students are being challenged in all of the ways that critics of our schools have urged that they be challenged, including opportunities to engage in active learning, acquisition of advanced problem-solving skills, and learning to work in teams. These students are seriously engaged in learning, they have parents who are strongly supportive of their efforts, and, for the most part, they find at least some teachers who are able to guide their achievements. These students are headed to our best colleges and universities and it is not surprising that both parents and students are highly satisfied with their schools.

In contrast to the performance of the most engaged students, there is ample evidence that a substantial proportion of American students—as many as 50 percent or more—do not work up to their academic potential, are indifferent about their academic performance, and are more interested in other things, such as sports and social activities. In a 1997 survey conducted by the Public Agenda, two-thirds of American teenagers admitted that they could do much better in school if they tried. Half of them said that their schools failed to challenge them to do their best (Public Agenda 1997). Fewer than half of the students in nine high schools surveyed in 1996 reported taking their studies seriously and 80 percent of

Avoiding Engagement

Her name was Melissa. She entered the classroom alone, yet still seemed easily a part of the mob of kids arriving for the English class. This was a college-track group of seniors in a large Midwestern city high school, one enrolling students from a wide mix of lower-income, working, and middle-class families.

Looking at no one in particular, Melissa headed toward a desk to the teacher's left, against the wall. She toted a large pile of texts and notebooks in front of her, slung between outstretched arms. She backed into the chair and, swiveling, deposited the books on the tablet arm.

The chattering ceased, and the class—on the poetry of John Donne—started with a brief, lively lecture, spiced with anecdotes. The students listened, a few took notes. The teacher soon switched to a poem by Donne that had been read in class the day before. What did it mean? She pushed the questions out into the students.

Melissa watched all this without animation. A question was directed to her. She looked at the teacher with little change in expression. A pause. I don't understand. The teacher repeated the question, kindly, without reproach. Another pause. I don't know. Maybe Donne means . . . Melissa, speaking slowly, quietly, said something, a phrase using words earlier spoken during the teacher's lecture. It was enough to end the exchange, but not enough to provoke a counterquestion or a follow-up by the teacher. The next question went elsewhere.

Melissa's cautious impassivity was unremitting. Melissa, however unwittingly, was a master at nonengagement. She sat at the side. She didn't move much, thus drawing little attention to herself. She did not offer ideas to the class, but when questioned, parried to buy time and then answered with something just plausible and relevant enough to avoid being chided for inattention or remarked on for perceptiveness or judged for error. She did well enough on tests to be in this college-track group. She was an educational artful dodger of considerable skill.

Once she got the hang of dodging, school could be quite effortless. She did enough to pass; her attendance was satisfactory; she would surely get a diploma. However, she would not be inspired—she fended off that prospect—and what she gained about the stuff of academic life and about disciplined intellectual inquiry would be largely by chance.

Excerpt from *Horace's Compromise: The Dilemma of the American High School*, by Ted Sizer (Boston, Mass.: Houghton Mifflin, 1984), 161–63.

these students disagreed with the statement that it is important to get good grades in school (Steinberg, Brown, and Dornbusch 1996). Conservatively, this means that as many as a million and a half students graduate from high school each year having missed out on the opportunity to acquire the knowledge and skills needed to participate fully as workers and citizens in our increasingly complex and technological society.

Yet neither these students nor their parents are unhappy with their schools or their own accomplishments in school. In large part, this reflects the priorities that students and parents alike have set for themselves—priorities that rank educational achievement below other things, such as the development of social skills, sports, and even having a good time in school. From an academic perspective, these students are not well served by their schools, however satisfied they or their parents might be.

Finally, a significant minority of students—perhaps as many as 25 percent—is almost entirely disengaged from the educational system by the time they reach high school, and many of them drop out before finishing high school (U.S. Department of Education 2002). A disproportionate number of these students are in urban schools serving largely low-income, minority populations. These schools have consistently failed to engage most of their students, and few of these schools have been affected by school reform efforts, despite nearly four decades of concerted efforts by cities, states, and the federal government to bring about positive changes in inner-city schools (National Research Council 2003). While lack of engagement in learning can be a problem in elementary schools, there is evidence that the process of disengagement of significant numbers of students begins in earnest in middle school and continues through high school (Steinberg, Brown, and Dornbusch 1996; Marks 2000; Stipek 2002).

Evidence from recent international comparative studies provides clear support for the foregoing observations, particularly regarding the achievement of students at the extremes of the distribution of students in this country. "The best students in the U.S. do as well as anyone in the world," according to Barry McGaw, the deputy director for education for the Organization for Economic Cooperation and Development, the Paris-based group that conducted the most recent survey of fifteen-year-olds' achievement in thirty-two nations (Hoff 2001). In reading, for example, the study showed that "the gap between America's best readers and its worst is wider than in any other country." Twelve percent of U.S. fifteen-year-olds scored in the top 10 percent of the international sample; only six countries had a higher proportion at that level. But 18 percent of the U.S. test takers scored at or below the lowest performance level in the exam. Scores in mathematics and science show a similar, though somewhat less extreme, pattern. The international comparisons also show that U.S. students in general do as well as their counterparts at the elementary school level, but by eighth grade have fallen behind, particularly in mathematics (Organization for Economic Cooperation and Development 2000).

These results are in line with the findings of previous international studies, which demonstrate that the best schools in the United States are on a par with schools in the highest-performing countries in the world. The poor showing of a significant minority of American schools lowers this country's overall performance to the international mean. Results from the Third International Mathematics and Science Study, for example, revealed that achievement in wealthy suburban schools is comparable with that of leading nations, but that U.S. inner-city schools rank with the lowest-scoring countries (National Center for Education Statistics 1999).

LOOKING AHEAD

The criticisms raised about the performance of the nation's schools over the last two decades surely result from deep concerns about the apparent failure of schools that serve our most disadvantaged students, the 25 percent who are least engaged in learning. They also reflect awareness on the part of most professionals and many parents of how much better the majority of U.S. students could be doing were they to become more engaged in learning academic skills. The American economy may not be on the verge of imminent collapse due to inadequacies of the educational system, but it is clear that significant increases in academic achievement are unlikely so long as many of America's schoolchildren are either indifferent to school or alienated from it.

Over the last two decades or more, substantial resources have been devoted to finding ways to improve our schools without measurable results. At the same time, there is good evidence that the vast majority of American students are not working at anywhere near their capacity. The inescapable conclusion is that the approaches taken to school reform in recent years have missed the main target: namely, increasing student engagement in learning. Yet the *potential* for improvement in educational outcomes is still enormous. If ways could be found to increase the amount of effort that students spend on academic activities, even by a small amount, the effect on outcome measures seems likely to be very large indeed.

The dire forecasts of the imminent failure of our education system, and with it the U.S. economy, may have turned out to be overblown, but the world continues to change at a rapid pace and far more dangerous challenges to the nation have arisen recently. The National Commission's concerns about America's ability to compete in the global economy, the skills of the American workforce, and the education required for participation in our democratic society now have been supplemented, if not replaced, by tangible anxiety about the security of the nation. In the context of current threats of terrorism from abroad, Stephen R. Graubard's (1995) admonition about the risks of isolationism and its implications for our schools seems prophetic:

> The new inward-looking America . . . has not yet realized that neither its pop culture nor its consumerism—exports and imports—can serve to give it any lasting security in the post-communist world. The United States, like every other nation, is required to live by its wits, and it has yet to understand how much that depends upon its educational system. (Graubard 1995, x)

In the years ahead, the capacity of America to meet these challenges seems certain to depend on whether many more of its citizens—not just an elite minority—acquire the knowledge and intellectual skills necessary to participate as active members not only of our democratic society but also of the global community. From an individual perspective, moreover, there is no reason to believe that the knowledge and intellectual skills students are supposed to learn in school—including the capacity for independent learning, problem solving, and critical thinking—will be any less important for success in the future than they have been in the past. That so many young people are only sporadically engaged in acquiring these skills represents an enormous failure, not only of the schools but also of the society that prepares its young people for these schools, fails to support their intellectual accomplishments, and tolerates—indeed, venerates—their mediocre academic performance.

NOTE

1. These discouraging national statistics mask some mildly promising accomplishments. A recent Quality Counts report compiled by *Education Week* (2002) shows that

> Since the last administration of the state-level NAEP tests in math in 1996, seventeen states have made small but statistically significant gains in the percentage of students scoring at or above the "proficient" level in mathematics, with nine states making improvements in math in both the fourth and eighth grades. The new NAEP science results show that seven states had significant improvement in the percentage of eighth graders performing at or above proficient since 1996.

Even with these improvements, however, less than 30 percent of fourth- and eighth-grade students in the United States perform at or above the proficient level in mathematics and science. According to this report, in seventeen states, the class of 2002 will be required to pass an exit or end-of-course exam to graduate and some states are making efforts to improve the quality of teaching by improving programs for new teachers and stiffening testing requirements for prospective teachers.

At the level of individual schools and school systems, there are many examples across the country of what appear to be successful efforts to increase student performance even under the most difficult circumstances, at least in the short term. (See, for example, Wagner's description of Central Park East Secondary School in New York City, 2002.) Of the major programs designed to foster the implementation of systematic reform models, several have generated enough positive results in well-designed evaluation studies to be judged "successful" or "promising," although none of these programs has as yet achieved these results in more than a few hundred schools (Herman et al. 1999).

❷

ENGAGEMENT: A NECESSARY
CONDITION FOR LEARNING

Learning requires engagement on the part of the learner. So far, no one has discovered a way to impart skills or knowledge without engaging the attention of the learner in some fashion. Although generations of students have gone to sleep with a textbook under their pillows, hoping against hope that some knowledge might find its way into their minds during the night, and there are sporadic reports of attempts to induce learning by playing tape recordings during sleep or through hypnosis, those who pursue these avenues awake disappointed in the morning. The search for truly effortless learning is doomed to fail. This simple truth underlies many of the ideas contained in the following pages.

What is engagement? The words that come readily to mind when we try to describe engagement in learning involve the investment of energy or effort on the part of the learner. They include paying attention, listening, concentrating, trying to remember, mentally rehearsing, thinking, and practicing. It is generally assumed that the more difficult the skill or knowledge to be acquired, the more effort is required to learn it; although true, this relationship is more complex than it appears. Everyone, for example, engages in what looks, at first glance, like nearly effortless learning when learning to talk—perhaps the most difficult learning task that anyone undertakes in the course of his or her life.

Despite the appearance of effortlessness, however, infants invest considerable energy into the task of learning language (as do their parents). More obviously, acquiring the physical and mental skills necessary to play the piano reasonably well requires a great deal of effort, expended over a relatively long period of time, no matter what one's age when one starts to learn.

The words used to describe engagement in learning suggest that there are several distinct dimensions to the concept. First, the learner must be *paying attention* to whatever it is that is to be learned. Second, as just noted, some *energy* must be expended. Third, the energy must be *directed* or channeled toward learning, so the learner is usually conscious of the task at hand. Fourth, engagement in learning usually involves *activity*, either mental or physical, such as practice, rehearsal, or repetition. And, finally, the effort usually must be expended *over time*; the learning of complex skills or knowledge rarely takes place instantly. In sum, engagement in learning implies a psychological investment on the part of the learner that includes, centrally, the expenditure of focused effort over some period of time (Newman, Wehlage, and Lamborn 1992).

Making the effort required to learn something can be enjoyable, but often it is not. Acquiring the skills necessary to participate in sports and other recreational activities involves many hours of hard work and practice, just like learning a foreign language or how to do advanced mathematics. When something is especially difficult, people rarely talk about how much fun it was to learn, usually settling for "satisfying" and the feeling of accomplishment that accompanies the realization that one has learned something new or gained a new skill.

Acquiring complex skills is not a linear process. Different stages of the learning process may require different levels of effort and may be more or less difficult or frustrating. In many instances, attaining a specific level or threshold may require special effort and, especially, perseverance. Once at such a threshold, however, both the pace and ease of learning may increase rapidly. This phenomenon can be seen readily in the acquisition of many physical skills from bike riding to wind surfing. In such cases, the learner has the experience of progressing from not being able to perform to feeling that he or she has acquired the requisite skill, if only at a minimal level, essentially in a single trial.

If a learner is committed to making the necessary effort, there is evidence that almost any method of instruction or learning environment "works," even one where others, such as teachers, play an insignificant role. Good teaching can facilitate learning, just as bad teaching can impede it. In fact, however, it is difficult to prevent people from learning things that they wish to learn. At the same time, it is clear that the context in which learning occurs can and often does have a powerful effect on a learner's inclination to engage in learning.

Viewed from this perspective, those who would seek to promote learning have three main tasks: (1) to induce prospective learners to become engaged, that is, to make the necessary psychological investment, including all of its dimensions; (2) to sustain their engagement, even when the going gets rough; and (3) to do everything possible to facilitate the learning process itself. What is involved in each of these aspects of the learning process?

STARTING THE ENGINE

What does it take to get the learning process started? First, as noted above, the learner must in some way become a participant in the process; he or she must become *engaged*. At a minimum, this means that the learner must be aware of his or her surroundings, and, specifically, those aspects of the environment that are pertinent to the learning task. For the infant who is beginning the task of learning to speak, this means that the child must be able to hear voices and differentiate them from other sounds. The easier this is for the infant and the more time (and energy) that is focused on this task, the more quickly the child will begin to make connections between specific sounds and events associated with those sounds. This all seems simple enough, but it raises a question: what causes the learner—the infant, in this case—to pay attention to its surroundings, and, within those surroundings, the voices it hears, in the first place? The answer seems to be that all human beings begin life with inherent, instinctual curiosity; they have a natural inclination to pay attention to their environment. Put another way, the engine that drives learning is already running, from the very beginning.

There is ample evidence that human beings naturally are curious about their surroundings almost from birth. Infants as young as a few days pay attention to movement and by the age of a few weeks will track a moving object within their field of vision. In addition, some types of objects or properties of objects are more interesting; for example, some colors (e.g., red) stimulate infants more than others. As they get older, children display interest in an increasing variety of things in their environment, paying particular attention to complex stimuli. These include, especially, the human beings who take care of them. Unless "turned off" by repeated negative reactions from the environment, the basic foundation for engagement in the learning process—namely, interest and curiosity—is in some manner "hardwired" into the human organism. Moreover, these characteristics of human beings seem to be linked to specific characteristics of the environment: the more complex the stimulus, the more likely it is to arouse interest on the part of the individual. From an evolutionary perspective, of course, there is nothing surprising about these facts about human beings.

People begin life as organisms that are programmed to pay attention to interesting things in their environment. As noted above, however, this is only the beginning of the learning process—an important but not necessarily sufficient precondition from a motivational perspective. For real learning to occur, attention must be sustained for some period of time, and energy must be invested in the learning process, whether consciously or unconsciously. (There is ample evidence, of course, that incidental learning does occur in the process of attending to what is going on around one. For example, people are often surprised that they remember having noticed something that they were not aware of at the time.) Early in the learning process, a subtle shift occurs from simply attending to things or events in one's environment to becoming engaged with them, beginning to make the psychological investment that sustains learning over time. This is where interaction between the learner and his or her surroundings becomes important and things begin to get complicated.

One of the most important principles governing the behavior of all organisms, including human beings, is that behavior that satisfies basic needs will tend to reoccur. Thus, simply speaking, individuals will be motivated to engage in activities that they find rewarding. Generally, rewards fall into two categories: (1) those that are intrinsic to the activities in which the individual engages (eating food that one likes when one is hungry or playing a game that is "fun") and (2) those that are extrinsic to the activity (receiving praise or some other reward, such as money, that is unrelated per se to the activity). While these two types of reward are conceptually distinct, in reality they are often intermingled in any particular activity. Moreover, what is rewarding at one point in time, or for any particular individual, frequently changes. Thus, food is a powerful reward, and therefore a source of motivation, when one is very hungry, but ineffective when one is sated. A computer game may be so intrinsically rewarding initially that it generates what looks like addictive behavior on the part of some individuals, but loses its motivating power once it has been mastered.

Rewards, be they intrinsic or extrinsic or some mixture of both, clearly are crucial to the process by which a prospective learner becomes engaged in any learning task. The sounds and accompanying gestures an infant's parents make when they talk to him serve to attract his or her attention. The rewards the child receives for beginning to emulate those sounds help to create and then sustain the motivation to engage in the extraordinarily difficult task of learning to talk. For some tasks, simply getting the engine running is enough to virtually ensure that sufficient learning will occur. For most kinds of learning, however, sustaining the learner's engagement in what often may be an arduous task is a formidable challenge.

KEEPING THE ENGINE RUNNING

Consider the example of learning to play the piano. By its nature, the piano is an intrinsically interesting machine that attracts the attention of almost anyone who has an opportunity to interact with it. Put almost any child in front of the keyboard of a piano and he or she will immediately become engaged in "playing" it. Moreover, a piano is sufficiently complex and interesting that it will sustain most children's engagement for a significant length of time—from tens of minutes to hours—and has the capacity to rekindle this engagement at periodic intervals, without any extrinsic rewards at all.

But, except for an occasional prodigy, children do not learn to play the piano as a result of random interaction with the instrument.

Becoming even a run-of-the-mill pianist requires both the acquisition of a set of very complex motor skills and, usually, mastery of a considerable body of knowledge about music in general, as well as the capacity to utilize this knowledge in specific instances (e.g., reading music and translating it into movements of one's fingers). Acquiring these skills and knowledge is hard work for most people, requiring a great deal of practice and study, usually over a relatively long period of time. What sustains the engagement necessary to accomplish this formidable learning task?

In the case of learning to play the piano, it is clear that the act of making music, even if the music is not very good at first, is powerfully and intrinsically rewarding for some students. Other pupils require constant encouragement and other forms of reward (or threats of punishment) in order to keep them engaged in the learning task. The engagement of most people who attempt to master the piano is sustained over time, therefore, by a complex mixture of intrinsic and extrinsic rewards, including the inherent pleasure of making music, the satisfaction that is associated with accomplishing something difficult, and rewards or threats of negative sanctions from parents, teachers, and other significant figures. As most parents of children who are taking piano lessons will attest, sustaining their engagement and motivation is not always an easy process, particularly when the tasks are difficult and progress is perceived by the learner to be slow.

Learning to play the piano may be viewed as a prototype for most, if not all, complex learning tasks. Although the things that affect both the initial and continued engagement of the learner are the same for any task, be it learning to read, play baseball or basketball, do algebra, or use a computer, their relative influence in every instance varies as a function of characteristics of the learner, the task, and the context in which learning is supposed to take place. These variables include, among others:

Characteristics of the learner

- inclination of the learner to undertake new learning, tackle difficult tasks, take risks
- expectations of the learner regarding the likelihood of success or failure

- perceptions of the learner of his or her abilities
- goals set by the learner for his or her performance

Characteristics of the task

- difficulty of the learning task
- how much learning is necessary before the learner begins to perceive that he or she is making progress
- the shape of the learning curve; that is, how rapidly learning is likely to take place at different points in the process
- the "fit" between characteristics of the learner and intrinsic, potentially rewarding properties of the learning task (e.g., does the piano student like music and possess natural musical abilities?)

Characteristics of the environment

- frequency of rewards for perseverance, success, from significant others, such as a teacher or parent
- assistance provided by others, such as a teacher
- negative sanctions for not paying attention, mistakes
- extent of distractions, competing activities

It should be noted that the word "teacher" appears in only two of the foregoing list of variables. This is not to imply that teachers are unimportant to the learning process. When one talks about characteristics of a good teacher, one usually emphasizes two important dimensions: first, the ability to explain things or present information in such a way as to make the learning process as easy as possible, and, second, to keep the learner fully engaged in the learning process. These two dimensions of learning clearly are related to one another. Sustaining engagement becomes impossible if the learner finds the task too difficult and is easier if the teacher can help the learner understand the task and see progress. But all good teachers know that engagement is a necessary condition for learning to occur. Teachers, of course, are in a position to affect nearly all of the variables listed above, and the best ones do so in ways designed to sustain the involvement of students in the learning process while simultaneously helping them learn.

MAKING LEARNING EASIER

The intricate relationship between engagement of the learner and characteristics of the learning task underscores the importance of structuring complex learning tasks in such a way as to maximize the chances that the learner will be rewarded for his or her efforts. "Structuring a learning task"—whether it be learning to read, do mathematics or advanced physics, play the piano, or swim—usually, but not always, involves dividing the task up into pieces of increasing difficulty so that the learner progresses from acquiring the simplest to successively more complex skills or understandings with relative ease. To give an obvious example, one does not assign beginning piano students a Beethoven sonata. This sounds simple, but since all learners do not approach the same learning task in the same way, it often turns out to be much more complicated in practice.

Teachers, parents, and other participants in the learning process often are involved in designing or adapting the learning progression to meet the needs of individual pupils. They also must help learners understand what is involved at each step, explain things that are confusing or otherwise difficult to understand, and, especially, encourage learners to engage in the practice necessary for them to take the next step in the progression (i.e., to sustain their engagement). Often, it is also necessary to take account of affective (noncognitive) factors such as fear of failure or even physical injury in the learning task. The tasks of learning to swim, ride a bicycle, or make a presentation in front of one's classmates all may engender feelings of anxiety on the part of learners that must be overcome before engagement can take place or in order for it to be sustained.

One of the classic problems in the design and implementation of educational curricula is striking the right balance between structuring specific learning tasks that are so easy that learners become bored and those that are so difficult that learners give up along the way. Finding this balance is especially difficult when the curriculum must be implemented simultaneously with a number of students of widely divergent abilities, preexisting knowledge and experiences, and interests. This is the challenge that classroom teachers face each day.

Designing curricula in such a way that "learners can proceed at their own pace" offers one approach to solving the foregoing problem. Conceptually, at least, increasingly sophisticated educational technologies enable pupils not only to progress in accordance with their own capabilities and energy but also to experiment with different cognitive learning strategies. In the absence of support (reinforcement) from teachers, parents, or peers, however, the technology itself must contain sufficiently powerful rewards to keep the learner engaged over time.

FACTORS THAT AFFECT ENGAGEMENT IN LEARNING: A CONCEPTUAL FRAMEWORK

Figure 2.1 summarizes many of the factors that can affect a learner's willingness to engage in and expend energy on learning, both initially and over time. As is readily apparent, the list of potentially relevant influences is long and complex. While the list is divided into four major categories—physiological, psychological, social/cultural, and task-related—for analytic purposes, in reality many of these variables are interrelated.

Physiological Factors

What are the essential preconditions for engagement in learning? In 1954, Albert Maslow advanced the theory that all human beings were subject to a hierarchy of needs, beginning with the most elemental physiological requirements of air to breathe, water, food, warmth, and procreation, up to a need for self-expression and creativity ("self-actualization," according to Maslow, the need for growth through the realization of one's potential and capacities; the need for comprehension and insight). The notion of a hierarchy of needs implies that unless essential needs at the lowest end of the scale are met, it is not realistic to expect humans to expend much effort on fulfilling higher-order needs. Thus, individuals who are hungry or thirsty or cold or sick cannot be expected to devote much energy to learning (unless they perceive that such an investment will make them less hungry or thirsty or cold or sick in the short term).

In establishing the school lunch program in 1946, the U.S. Congress took account of the fact that adequate nutrition is an important precondition for learning. These programs now benefit 26 million children

Figure 2.1. Factors That Affect Engagement in Leaning.

	Physiological	Psychological	Task-Related/ Educational	Social/Cultural	Learner Activities/ Engagement
Things that have positive effect	• General health/ well-being • Good nutrition • Adequate sleep • Fed and clothed	• Self-confidence; expectation that can succeed • Sense of mastery • Sense of control • Rational calculus that it's worth the effort • Meaningful rewards • Encouragement • Attention from significant others	• Cognitively appropriate • Appropriate level of difficulty • Perceived relevance of task/subject matter • Good pedagogy • Active learning • Interesting task/ subject matter • Sufficient time on task	• Family socialization: value of hard work, perseverance • Expectations of family support • Social support system • Extended family • Other adults • Role models • Peer group support	**Engagement** Paying attention Concentrating Trying to remember Mentally rehearsing Thinking Practicing Focus on task Perseverance
LEARNER Abilities					
Things that have negative effect	• Hunger • Fatigue • Cold or hot • Illness • Micronutritional deficiency • Poor general health; low energy • Parasites • Drugs/alcohol	• Expectation of failure; lack of confidence • Lack of control • Rational calculus that it's not worth the effort • Absence of rewards • Punishment, perceived failure, ridicule	• Boring task/ subject matter • Poor pedagogy • Passive learning • Too easy or difficult • Lack of perceived relevance • Insufficient time on task	• Lack of family, peer-group support • Negative role models • Competition for attention • TV • Sports • Social • Competing demands, expectations	

nationwide, but overall address only part of the nutritional deficits that a significant number of mainly poor children in this country face. (The implications of this point for the education of children in developing countries around the world are profound. Moreover, to general nutritional deficiencies must be added the effect of micronutritional deficiencies, parasites, and other illnesses that may be common in developing countries.)

Inadequate nutrition is only one of the health problems that are associated with inadequate family income in the United States. Children living in poor families are far more likely to suffer from a variety of health problems ranging from dental cavities and asthma to lead poisoning and attention deficit hyperactivity disorder (ADHD) than middle- and upper-class children. Poor children are also more likely to be admitted to a hospital and 15 percent of all children—most of them poor—are without health insurance. Inadequate prenatal care and maternal smoking also have been demonstrated to have a significant negative effect on academic performance (Rothstein 2002).

Adequate rest is another important consideration if schoolchildren are to have the energy they need to actively participate in the learning process. Recent studies have shown, for example, that school schedules requiring teenagers to get up very early in the morning have a significant negative impact on performance. A clear policy implication is that high schools should not begin before 8:30 or 9:00 A.M., especially if school bus routes are long.

A hundred years ago, a significant proportion of the children in the United States were required to work in addition to attending school, whether on farms or in factories. Child labor laws addressed this problem for younger children early in the last century but more recently, children's lives outside of school have been filled with more and more structured activities, many of which compete with school for a child's energy and attention.

Finally, the use of drugs and alcohol can have a significant negative effect on engagement in learning. Data on the use of drugs and alcohol by elementary and secondary school students in the United States suggest that both substances continue to be a major factor in the lives of a substantial proportion of our children. (See chapter 7 for current data on the use of drugs and alcohol by elementary and secondary school students.)

Psychological Factors

A long history of research on factors affecting motivation has demonstrated that a number of psychological variables have a powerful influence on an individual's motivation to engage in any particular task. Among the most important of these variables are those that affect the learner's expectation that he or she will be able to succeed at the learning task. The beliefs held by all of the participants about the relative importance of effort versus ability in learning have a major influence on learner expectations. If inherent abilities are viewed as especially important for success in learning, then it will be more difficult to convince learners to expend the necessary effort unless the learner perceives that he or she has the requisite ability. Parents and teachers, moreover, may be less inclined to establish high expectations for performance for learners whom they perceive as having lower levels of ability. The converse is likely to be true if effort is seen as determinative of achievement. American culture, while somewhat ambivalent on the issue of effort versus ability, has always placed great emphasis on natural abilities. In contrast, for example, Japanese culture attributes success almost exclusively to the amount of effort exerted. This characteristic of American society has had profound implications for our schools, as is discussed in chapter 3.

Related to a student's beliefs about the relative importance of effort versus ability is his or her sense of competence and control over the learning environment. Students are unlikely to become engaged in learning if they do not think they can succeed or if they perceive that they have no control over the outcome (National Research Council 2003).

Next are those variables that relate to the learner's expectation that effort will lead to a reward of some sort (or, in some cases, the avoidance of punishment). In the broadest sense, rewards and punishments generally are acknowledged to play a central role in learning and are an integral part of most strategies for motivating learners to participate actively in the learning process. Hence, teachers and parents routinely dispense praise (and sometimes more tangible rewards) for effort on the part of learners, as well as for the results of that effort. They also threaten pupils with various kinds of punishment if they fail to make the necessary effort. As noted above, some rewards may be intrinsic to the learning task itself or to the relationship between the task and the learner. An important goal of most teachers is to engage learners in a learning task to such an extent that extrinsic rewards are no longer necessary to sustain the learners' motivation.

Although the effect of rewards and punishments on motivation is conceptually straightforward, in practice the relationship is much more complex. There has been a great deal of debate, for example, about the relative efficacy of positive as opposed to negative sanctions for motivating learners. There is evidence that the threat of powerful negative sanctions can inhibit learning by creating high levels of anxiety on the part of at least some learners. Certain kinds of negative sanctions—for example, ridicule—can have long-lasting negative effects on the confidence of learners and their willingness to engage in learning in the future. Similarly, rewards that are extraneous to the learning task (for example, money) under some circumstances can distract learners from the task at hand by focusing all of their efforts on obtaining the reward.

To complicate matters further, the effect on the motivation of any particular individual of different kinds and levels of rewards and punishments is mediated by personality characteristics of that individual. Thus, some individuals respond well to challenges that involve significant risks of failure so long as the rewards are perceived to be great enough. Other individuals tend to be risk averse and require constant encouragement in order to sustain their motivation. Some individuals tend to approach tasks with confidence that they can succeed; others are more likely to anticipate failure. Some individuals are more capable than others of calculating the potential returns on energy invested in the short term and in sustaining their efforts despite lack of immediate rewards.

Finally, it is not always easy to predict in advance exactly what will be rewarding (or punishing) and therefore motivating to any particular individual. For some learners, the encouragement of significant others —peers, teachers, parents, other adults—is of crucial importance. For others, the perception that they are in fact learning something may be more motivating than any external reward. For those who achieve it, a sense of mastery of a subject or skill may be the most rewarding and therefore motivating experience of all.

In the context of schooling, it is apparent that one of the things that distinguishes good teachers is their ability to figure out how to use different mixtures of positive and negative sanctions that will be most effective in sustaining the engagement of each student in learning.

Task-Related Factors

The likelihood that a learner will become engaged and stay engaged in any learning task is influenced by several characteristics of the learning task itself. These include (1) the perceived level of difficulty of the task in relation to the learner's capabilities, (2) the extent to which the task is cognitively appropriate for the learner, (3) perceived high expectations for success from others, (4) the perceived relevance or irrelevance of the subject matter, (5) whether the learning task is structured in such a way as to actively involve the learner, (6) whether the learner perceives the task as inherently interesting or fun, and (7) the amount of time that can be spent on the task.

It is obvious that a learner is unlikely to become engaged seriously in any task that he or she perceives to be too difficult (or, for that matter, too easy) at the outset. Thus, despite some apocryphal stories, one does not attempt to teach children to swim by first asking them to jump into deep water, or a beginning piano student by giving him or her a Beethoven sonata to play, or a novice to ski by starting him or her at the top of the mountain. Every good teacher knows that the first step in getting a learner engaged in the learning process is to present the learner with a task that is manageable, given his or her existing capabilities. This is often not as simple as it may seem, since it requires the teacher to figure out exactly what the learner's capabilities are and to make appropriate adjustments in the learning progression to take these capabilities into account. Although there is usually an opportunity to correct for mistakes in judgment about a learner's capabilities, failure to notice that a learner is overmatched by a learning task, or conversely, finds the task too easy, can have long-lasting negative effects. Getting the progression right for every child in a class of thirty or more children is a formidable challenge indeed. There is a growing body of evidence, however, that high expectations for performance on the part of teachers are essential for student motivation and engagement in learning, so long as students do not regard such expectations as entirely unrealistic. Most students want and need to be challenged, so long as demands are viewed as fair and achievable.

In addition to the relationship between the difficulty of learning tasks and capabilities of the learner, recent research in cognitive science has provided evidence that different individuals bring different experiences, understandings, and cognitive styles to each learning task. The way that a learning task is structured, therefore, can affect the propensity of learners to engage in it. A key insight into how children learn, for example, is that learners build new knowledge on the framework of existing knowledge. When new knowledge is consistent with existing concepts, it supports learning. When it conflicts with existing concepts, it may hamper learning (National Research Council 1999).

Another factor that can influence the propensity of students to engage in the learning process is the extent to which the skills and information being imparted are perceived by the learner as relevant in any way to his or her life. Skills and information may be seen as immediately relevant and useful, or they may be seen as necessary for the achievement of some future goal, such as graduating from high school or gaining entrance to college. Young people differ, of course, in their abilities to internalize and act based upon future goals, especially those that may seem remote in time or the likelihood that they can be achieved.

Learning tasks may be structured in such a way as to require the active involvement of the learner, or they may allow the learner to remain passive. Lectures, demonstrations, and reliance on media-based presentations may or may not engage the attention of students; in any case, the learner remains essentially passive. In contrast, a variety of pedagogical techniques—from the Socratic method to project-based learning—actively involve the learner in the process. There is ample evidence that the active involvement of the learner increases his or her engagement.

Some learning tasks are intrinsically engaging, at least for some period of time. In the late 1950s, Yale sociologist Omar K. Moore successfully made use of the inherently engaging character of an electric typewriter to teach very young children to read by encouraging them to explore the typewriter's keyboard. Today, any parent can testify to the powerfully engaging qualities of computer-based games. Harnessing these qualities in the service of school-related learning has been the focus of a new industry devoted to increasing the use of technology in education, so far with mixed success. Within the traditional curriculum, it is clear that the majority of pupils gravitate naturally to some subjects as opposed to others—for example, literature, science, and social studies as opposed to mathematics or foreign languages.

Finally, the amount of time a learner can spend on any particular learning task is of critical importance. "Time on task" is directly related to all measures of achievement and even the most motivated and engaged student will not succeed in learning if he or she is unable to spend the time necessary for learning to occur. This point, while obvious, takes on special importance when one considers the way most American schools are organized and the amount of instructional time available to pupils in a normal school day.

Social and Cultural Factors

Learning always occurs in a social context. Even when a learner is practicing or studying alone, or sitting at a computer, a host of contextual influences, both past and present, play an important role in sustaining the learner's engagement in any learning task. These variables include the impact of significant others, including family and peer group members as well as other adults and role models outside the family, and a wide range of things that compete for the learner's attention in the present time. All of the variables are mediated by the cultural context within which learning occurs.

A child's first learning experiences occur within the family, and parents (as well as siblings) play a crucial role in shaping and then reinforcing a child's responses to the challenges of acquiring new skills and knowledge throughout the first years of life. Children who are encouraged to engage in learning tasks and who are rewarded for perseverance, whether or not they succeed, are more likely to engage in such activities in the future. On the other hand, children who are punished for failure quickly learn that engagement carries with it risks, which they can avoid by not participating in the first place.

Families also set expectations for their children and every parent (and teacher) faces the challenge of finding the right balance between setting expectations so high that the child becomes discouraged or so low that the child is not sufficiently challenged. As an individual's capabilities change and grow, moreover, expectations must constantly be modified.

In addition to encouraging and reinforcing specific behaviors, as well as setting expectations, significant others within and outside the family serve as powerful role models for children. The way in which parents, other relatives, older siblings, influential adults outside the family, and peers approach new tasks can have a profound influence on the way children approach them. Children who are surrounded by friends and family members who demonstrate high motivation and a willingness to engage in learning a variety of new tasks over time will themselves be more likely to become engaged in learning. Conversely, it is likely to be more difficult to generate and sustain the motivation of children who have not had the benefit of positive role models, or who are exposed to negative models.

Parents, in particular, play a unique role in transmitting to their children attitudes, beliefs, and values about the importance of academic achievement and the behaviors necessary to succeed in school. Hard work, perseverance, self-discipline, and respect for authority are among the values that are essential for sustained academic achievement; internalization of these values depends to a large extent on the influence of parents. In thinking about the role of parents, moreover, it is important to recognize the existence of cultural differences in the attitudes and values of parents regarding the importance of academic achievement.

Finally, account must be taken of an array of contextual influences that may strengthen or diminish an individual's motivation to engage in learning in any specific instance. One of the most important is the extent to which there are competing demands for the learner's attention and energies. Sports, television, video and computer games, hobbies, and the lure of social activities associated with peer groups all compete for the attention of young people. In rare instances, these influences may serve to reinforce a learner's engagement; in most cases, they divert energy away from school-related learning.

CONCLUSIONS AND CAVEATS

Before turning to a detailed consideration of the foregoing factors that influence a student's engagement in learning, some caveats and conclusions are in order. First, although conceptually it is possible to make distinctions among the things that influence engagement in learning, many of these factors are, in fact, interrelated. Second, while engagement ultimately occurs at the level of the individual, the main objective in the pages that follow is to identify things that are likely to make a difference for most young people. There is no doubt that the interaction between a particular student and his or her teacher can and frequently does make a great deal of difference in the student's willingness to engage in the learning process. This fact does not make consideration of things that can affect the engagement of many students any less important.

Third, while it is apparent that many things affect engagement in learning, both positively and negatively, underlying much of the discussion is the notion that most students begin with a natural inclination to engage in learning. What is remarkable is the resilience of this inclination and how difficult it is to extinguish. Fourth, the preceding observation, coupled with an awareness of the range of things that can increase an individual's willingness to engage in learning, underscores a point made in chapter 1: namely, that there exists an enormous opportunity to dramatically increase the output of the nation's schools. If the very large number of students who are at present doing only what is necessary to get by could be enticed into increasing their engagement in learning, even by a modest amount, the results would be impressive indeed.

3

EFFORT VERSUS ABILITY:
A MATTER OF EXPECTATIONS

It is widely understood and accepted by professionals and most other members of American society that both individual effort and innate abilities play important roles in all learning. Most cultures recognize the existence of inherited differences in the ability of individuals to acquire knowledge and skills, both academic and nonacademic. It is readily accepted, for example, that some people are naturally talented dancers, musicians, athletes, artists, or writers. Just as some people are genetically endowed to grow to be taller, stronger, or more adept physically, so too do some inherit greater mental capacity or intelligence than others. There is accumulating evidence, moreover, that different kinds of mental abilities may also be influenced by one's genetic makeup. Thus, for example, some children may have the ability to learn mathematical concepts more quickly than others while some children inherit greater linguistic capabilities.

A great deal of research has been done over the last half century on the relative contribution of inherited capabilities and individual effort to a wide range of intellectual and other achievements. Although significant disagreements remain among scientists on this matter, four important facts stand out.

- First, there is no doubt that both innate characteristics and individual effort play important roles in the capacity of humans to acquire most knowledge and skills.
- Second, it is clear that no matter how great or limited an individual's inherent abilities, whatever potential the individual has will remain unrealized without effort on his or her part. The more effort that is expended, the more likely it is that an individual's inherited potential will be realized.
- Third, inherited abilities matter most at the extremes. Both individuals with severe limitations in their capacity to learn and those with extraordinary capabilities present special challenges for parents, teachers, and schools. For the majority of us, however, inherited differences in intellectual capacity (or, for that matter, other abilities) matter far less than differences in the amount of effort we are prepared to exert in order to learn.
- Fourth, at least as important as actual differences in inherited capabilities are the beliefs that we hold about them and the influence of these beliefs on our behavior, in particular on our willingness to expend the effort necessary to learn.

This fourth point is the primary focus of this chapter.

BELIEFS ABOUT THE IMPORTANCE OF EFFORT VERSUS INNATE ABILITY

Every culture incorporates beliefs about the factors that contribute to acquiring the knowledge and skills necessary for successful performance of important roles in the society. These beliefs serve as guides for parents, teachers, and others responsible for socializing new members of the society, as well as for those being socialized (e.g., children). Among the most important of these beliefs are those concerning the relationship between effort and accomplishment. Although most societies and cultures acknowledge that success in school is the product of a combination of effort and innate ability, the relative emphasis placed on effort as opposed to ability differs significantly from one society to another (Peak 1993).

A fundamental tenet of American culture is the belief that anyone can succeed if he or she tries hard enough. This belief is reflected in the importance Americans attach to education, its role in society, and the conviction that it is through education that one can improve one's station in life, and, especially, that of one's children. At the same time, however, since the first part of the twentieth century, Americans have been fascinated by the concept of innate intelligence. Following the work of French psychologist Alfred Binet and his colleague Theodore Simon, Lewis Terman developed the first standardized test of intelligence in 1916. The Stanford-Binet, as it was called, introduced the notion of a ratio between mental age and chronological age (the Intelligence Quotient or IQ) as a way of expressing test results (Goslin 1963).

From the beginning, American psychologists and educators enthusiastically embraced the idea that intelligence could easily be measured and, moreover, that it was a measure of innate abilities. One of the first uses of IQ tests envisioned by Terman and other psychologists at that time was as a way of determining which children could succeed at different occupations requiring different levels of intelligence. As Lauren Resnick and others have pointed out, "early in this century, we built an education system around the assumption that aptitude is paramount in learning and that it is largely hereditary. The system was oriented toward selection, distinguishing the naturally able from the less able and providing students with programs thought suitable to their talents" (Resnick 1995, 56).

The stage was set, therefore, for a conflict between two important beliefs in American society—the necessity of hard work for success in life and the central importance of innate abilities. This conflict continues to be reflected in how most people think about the achievement of individuals in our society, as well as in many current institutional policies and practices. There is little doubt, for example, that beliefs about the importance of inherited abilities still pervade our culture. In the early 1960s, a team of researchers at the Russell Sage Foundation in New York conducted one of the few studies of the beliefs held by students, parents, teachers, guidance counselors, and the public at large about intelligence and its relevance to academic achievement (Brim 1969; Goslin 1967). Among adults and secondary school teachers in a national sample, 25 percent expressed the view that IQ tests measure mostly inborn intelligence, while nearly 40 percent of secondary school counselors and elementary school teachers expressed that opinion (Goslin 1967, 58). When public school teachers were asked in the same study which of several kinds of information provided the single most accurate measure of a student's intellectual ability, almost 40 percent chose IQ or scholastic aptitude test scores. Slightly more than 25 percent chose achievement test scores and 15 percent selected grades as the best indicator of ability (Brim 1969).

Two decades later, Harold Stevenson and James Stigler (1992) asked fifth-graders in Sendai, Taipei, and Minneapolis to rate the degree to which they agreed or disagreed with the following statement: "The tests you take can show how much or how little natural ability you have." Chinese and Japanese children "were less likely than American children to accept the proposal that tests can reveal natural ability." When mothers were asked to rate the importance of effort, ability, difficulty of task, and luck for their child's performance in school, all three groups ranked effort first, but American mothers gave significantly more points to ability than the other two groups. Stevenson and Stigler conclude: "No matter how we asked the questions or to whom we directed them, the answers were consistent: Americans were more likely to assign greater importance to innate ability than were Chinese or Japanese."

Americans' beliefs in the importance of innate abilities are reflected in a variety of important policies and practices that, taken together, reinforce an ability-based model of education in this country (Resnick 1995). These policies include the widespread use of IQ tests to select children for gifted and talented programs, as well as the practice of grouping children according to their abilities for instructional purposes in classrooms. Scores on most standardized tests continue to be based on how well students perform in comparison with others, and many teachers grade students on a curve, thereby ensuring that as many as half of the students in each class are not rewarded for their efforts. Finally, admission to many colleges and universities is heavily influenced by scores applicants make on the Scholastic Aptitude Test (SAT) (despite some recent calls for its discontinuation or modification).

At the same time, since the early 1990s, the country has espoused a national standards-based reform movement based on the principle that all students should be expected to meet high academic standards oriented around challenging subject matter, the acquisition of higher-order thinking skills, and the application of abstract knowledge to solving real-world problems (McLaughlin and Shepard 1995). Unlike many previous reform efforts, a major goal of the standards-based movement is the development and implementation of new curricular materials and assessment systems designed to ensure that teachers have the necessary knowledge and tools to monitor and increase the accomplishments of all students. Recent passage of the No Child Left Behind Act of 2001 represents an important step in this movement toward establishing expectations that most, if not all, children can meet high standards in school.

Reconciliation of these conflicting sets of beliefs and the policies that derive from them present an important challenge for the society. It is clear that beliefs about the relative contribution of inherited abilities and individual effort to learning held by parents, teachers, school counselors, and other significant persons in children's lives help to shape and reinforce children's views about their abilities and, most important, expectations for future learning. Positive expectations on the part of teachers or parents regarding a child's capacity to learn have been shown to be associated with greater achievement (Stipek 2002; Pintrich and Schunk 1996; Weinstein 1993). Conversely, negative expectations regarding abilities and therefore performance are associated with lower achievement. The central question is whether parents, teachers, and others can find ways to convey positive expectations regarding the performance of all children, while simultaneously taking into account the existence of individual differences in abilities.

The mechanisms by which expectations are translated into higher or lower achievement on the part of children include the transmittal of cues that help shape a child's self-image, as well as behaviors that reinforce his or her engagement in learning. What are the sources of children's beliefs about their own abilities?

CHILDREN'S BELIEFS ABOUT THEIR ABILITIES

It is reasonable to assume that every learner approaches every learning task with a set of beliefs about the relative importance of effort versus ability as a determinant of successful performance, and an estimate of his or her own ability to succeed at the task. For very young children, beliefs about the relationship between effort and innate abilities are unlikely to be well formed, but there is evidence that even during early elementary grades, children have distinct beliefs about the kinds of things that they are good at (Wigfield and Eccles 1994, 2001). As individuals gain experience with different learning tasks and their own performance, as well as with others' beliefs and expectations about and for them, their own beliefs and perceptions of self become more refined.

Many of the cues children use to make inferences about both their abilities and the importance of effort are straightforward. They include comments of parents, teachers, and peers, as well as direct experience of successful or unsuccessful performance under varying conditions of effort. The beliefs of both adults and children also are influenced in important ways by observations of the accomplishments of others, both in school and in a variety of other settings, and by culturally shaped assumptions about the factors that contribute to those accomplishments.

The accomplishments of outstanding athletes, musicians, writers, or artists, in addition to scientists, mathematicians, and other academicians, may be attributed to great (presumably inherited) talent or hard work or both. The greater the accomplishments (or, conversely, the more conspicuous the lack of accomplishment) or the speed with which a skill is learned, however, the more the performance is likely to be attributed to innate abilities. Thus, truly extraordinary academic performance is associated with the term "genius," children who demonstrate exceptional musical or artistic accomplishments at an early age are described as "prodigies," and an outstanding athlete may be referred to as a "natural." All three terms, which are deeply imbedded in our culture, carry a strong connotation of innate ability. At the other end of the spectrum of ability, individuals who have difficulty learning are likely to be labeled as "dumb" or "retarded," also terms suggesting that the condition is inherited.

As children are developing beliefs about the relative importance of effort as compared with innate abilities for learning, they are also forming estimates of their own capacity to perform in different domains. As with their beliefs, the sources of these self-estimates are varied and often complex, both direct and indirect. One of the most important influences on children's knowledge about their own abilities is the differential treatment of both themselves and others that they perceive in school (Weinstein 1993). At least eight different aspects of classroom and school practice have been identified as having the potential to serve as sources of information to children about their abilities:

1. grouping practices
2. the system for assigning tasks within the classroom
3. the strategies teachers choose to motivate their students
4. the extent to which students are expected to take responsibility for their own learning
5. the various ways in which feedback is provided to students on their performance
6. the quality of relationships that teachers have with each student
7. opportunities for participation in school activities outside the classroom
8. the extent of parent involvement

In each of these instances, the potential exists for teachers and others involved in the classroom to treat children with high and low abilities differently. Weinstein notes that there now exists "substantial evidence that children (even as young as first graders) are aware of differential treatment by teachers toward high and low achievers" (Weinstein 1993, 199).

For most children, the effect of the information they receive about their abilities from teachers, classmates, and others is to lower their perceptions of their own abilities. Numerous studies have shown that children's self-perceptions of academic ability decline as they get older and are able to compare their own performance with that of others, as well as objective measures, such as grades and test scores. As students progress through the educational system, moreover, the comparative basis for their judgments about their abilities becomes broader and broader. As Stipek (2002) notes:

Elementary school students compare themselves primarily with their classmates. In junior high, students begin to pay attention to track placement and grade point averages, which can be compared schoolwide. By the final years of high school, outcomes of scholarship competitions, college admissions, and other indicators of achievement relative to national norms figure into some students' judgments of their competence. Analogous changes are likely to apply to athletic and other spheres of performance. The shift toward using normative criteria to judge ability is a major factor in the average decline of children's ratings of their ability from the early grades to high school. (87)

As children incorporate information that they receive from teachers and others about their own abilities and those of their peers, these self-estimates interact with emergent beliefs about the relative importance of effort versus ability in complex ways. Sharon Nelson-LeGall (1993) summarized some of the relevant research as follows:

> From the time of school entry and on into the primary grade level, children view effort as an important, and perhaps the most important, determinant of achievement outcomes (Surber 1984). Greater achievement is judged to be due to greater effort and greater effort is taken as a sign of greater ability. With increasing age and schooling, however, judgments of ability become related to judgments of effort in a (more complex) causal schema such that, for some students and in some academic achievement settings, trying harder comes to imply lesser ability and greater achievement is more likely to be explained by greater ability than by greater effort. (Nicholls and Miller 1984, 226)

Graham and Weiner (1993) argue that this inversion of the perceived relationship between effort and ability is more likely when the source of the information is a teacher (or, presumably, a parent) who wishes to protect the self-esteem of a failure-prone student. Examples of such well-intentioned teacher behaviors that may function indirectly as negative cues about ability include expressions of pity following failure, praise following success on easy tasks, and unsolicited offers of help.

With respect to the first of these unintentional cues, Graham and Weiner (1993) note that student failure perceived (by teachers) as caused by low ability is likely to elicit pity or sympathy in teachers, whereas failure due to lack of effort is more likely to generate anger. Students make use of these cues in formulating judgments about their own abilities (Graham 1984). Similarly, praise can lead to inferences upon the part of students of high effort, which is in turn associated with

lower perceived ability. Blame, on the other hand, typically is associated with low effort and, therefore, with perceptions of higher ability.
For example, frequent blame or criticism for the quality of one's work
was shown to be positively related to higher self-concept of math ability and high future expectations among students (Parsons, Kaczala, and
Meece 1982).

Finally, there is evidence that teacher help versus neglect can indirectly function as a low-ability cue, particularly when the help is unsolicited by the student. Graham is careful to emphasize that the foregoing teacher behaviors do not always function as low-ability cues, with
negative consequences for low-ability students. This line of research and
theory, however, provides further evidence of the complexity of
processes by which individuals form beliefs about their abilities and the
potential consequences of these beliefs for engagement in learning.

BELIEFS ABOUT ABILITY AND
ENGAGEMENT IN LEARNING

It is clear that the sources of self-estimates of ability and beliefs about
the relative importance of ability versus effort in achievement are complex. Equally complex are the processes through which these beliefs
and ability estimates affect the inclination of individuals to engage in
learning. On the surface, the relationship appears to be simple: children who (a) perceive themselves as having the ability to learn a particular skill, (b) recognize that effort is required to learn it, and (c) attach value to engagement in the learning task, either because it is
intrinsically interesting or because they perceive that they will be rewarded for accomplishing it, will be motivated to engage in the learning task. Conversely, children who (a) believe that they do not have the
requisite ability and (b) do not believe that their exertion of effort will
make up for their lack of ability will be disinclined to engage in the
learning task, irrespective of promised rewards or threatened punishments. On a simple risk-benefit calculation, they conclude that the risk
of failure (with its attendant unpleasant consequences) is too high to
warrant the expenditure of the necessary energy. Such a straightforward rational calculus obviously accounts for many decisions on the

part of learners not to engage in learning. Much of the time, however, such decisions are influenced by a number of additional factors.

The Expectations and Encouragement Paradox

Learners often are uncertain about whether they have the ability to succeed. This is usually the case with very young children who may not have formulated beliefs about their own abilities. It is also often the case when the learning task is different from anything the learner has experienced in the past (for example, learning a foreign language for the first time, beginning algebra or physics, or playing the piano). And, of course, it is likely to be the case when the task is perceived from the outset as being very difficult.

Under any of the foregoing circumstances, reassurance and encouragement are often required to persuade the learner to make the necessary effort: reassurance that the learner has the requisite abilities to succeed, and encouragement to make the effort. One of the things that parents and teachers routinely do with their children and students is to assure them that they have the ability to succeed if they are willing to make the effort. In a culture where all children are assumed to have more or less the same ability, and where effort is viewed as the main determinant of achievement, this kind of encouragement is likely to have the desired effect. In a culture that places more emphasis on innate abilities, however, such assurances can increase the potential negative consequences of failure in the mind of the learner because they create expectations that ultimately will be connected to judgments about the learner's abilities. Thus, telling children how smart they are, or what great tennis players they are going to be, can create disincentives to engage in the learning process because the child may be afraid of failing to live up to his or her parents' or teachers' expectations, not to mention discovering that he is not as smart or as talented as he thought or hoped he might be. For some children, the solution to this problem is to avoid engagement in learning.

Social Status, Self-image, and the Concept of Innate Abilities

In societies that are characterized by a strong belief in the existence and importance of innate abilities for achievement, such as our own, high ability is often associated with high status, and therefore with positive self-esteem. In the United States, it is much better to have a reputation as an "intelligent," "bright," or "smart" child than it is to be regarded as "a grind." Since hard work can be associated with negative assumptions about an individual's abilities ("he can't be very smart if he works so hard") and consequently also with status, many able students consciously strive to avoid giving their peers the impression that they work hard in school. This helps to explain why some of the most able students expend so little effort on academic achievement in school.

For students who believe that ability is the primary reason for success in school and, conversely, that failure is due to lack of ability, maintaining a positive image of their own ability (and, therefore, self-worth) depends crucially on avoiding failure (Covington 1992, in Alderman 1999). Many adolescents, in particular, adopt a variety of strategies to minimize the risk of failure (Stipek 2002). These include (1) deliberately minimizing the amount of effort they expend on any learning task (thus preserving the excuse that they could have succeeded if they had worked harder), (2) avoiding engagement in the task altogether (it was boring or "I forgot to do it"), and (3) self-handicapping behaviors, such as procrastination or setting goals that are impossible to achieve (Alderman 1999).

Sustaining Engagement in Learning

The pervasiveness of an ability-based model of learning in this country has implications for the willingness of individuals to stay engaged in learning in many situations, not just in school. In American culture, one of the first explanations for failure often is lack of innate ability, which may lead to disengagement. In sports, for example, many young people (not to mention adults) quickly become discouraged if they do not immediately display natural abilities, even when the required skills are complex and difficult. Coaches who pay more attention to their best players can reinforce this outcome.

An effort-based model of learning, in contrast, places more emphasis on persistence, which can help all students gain more skill and confidence. In a recent study, for example, Carol Dweck (2000) found that students who believe that intelligence is changeable over time earned

Behaviors Reflecting Perceptions of Ability and Self-Efficacy

Students who are self-confident in the ability to succeed:

- approach tasks eagerly
- persist in the face of failure
- seek help after they have tried on their own
- enjoy and choose challenging work
- volunteer to answer questions and provide answers when called on
- help other students
- show pride in their work

Students who lack self-confidence in their ability to succeed:

- say things like "I can't" and "It's too hard"
- attribute success to external causes, such as help or luck
- prefer easy work that can be done without much effort
- are easily discouraged or distracted
- give up easily
- seek help without trying, or don't seek help when they need it
- don't volunteer answers to questions
- volunteer to answer questions and then "forget" their answer
- change assignments to something they can do
- claim that the work is boring
- make excuses for not completing work
- procrastinate, then claim that they didn't have time
- "overstrive," that is, review over and over; rewrite and rewrite
- obsess; have difficulty "letting go" of work

From: Deborah Stipek, *Motivation to Learn: Integrating Theory and Practice* (Boston, Mass.: Allyn and Bacon, 2002), 92.

better grades and expressed more enthusiasm about their school work than those who believe intelligence is fixed. These students were also rated by their teachers as "more diligent, focused, and persistent, as well as harder workers."

In their comparison of Asian and American students' approach to mathematics learning, Stevenson and Stigler (1992) observed that American students have a tendency to view learning mathematics as a process of rapid insight rather than lengthy struggle, a perspective that is consistent with an ability-based model of learning and accomplishment. As a result, American children have a tendency to give up if they encounter difficult problems. In contrast, Asian students are more likely to assume they can figure out the solution if they persevere. In a test of this hypothesis, American and Asian children were asked to solve as many mathematics problems as they could within a time limit of twenty minutes. The result was revealing.

> Japanese children attempted the fewest problems and American children attempted the most. Of those problems that were attempted, however, the highest percentage of correct answers at first grade was in Japan (85 percent), the next in Taiwan (75 percent) and the lowest was in Chicago (61 percent). In fifth grade, the pattern was similar: both Chinese and Japanese students solved about 77 percent of the problems they attempted; American students solved only 51 percent. The American children's strategy of skipping rapidly across the problems did not pay off; they solved a smaller percentage of the problems they attempted, and their overall number of correct answers was also significantly below that of the Asian children.

Stevenson and Stigler conclude:

> In sum, the relative importance people assign to factors beyond their control, like ability, compared to factors that they can control, like effort, can strongly influence the way they approach learning. Ability models subvert learning through the effects they have on the goals that parents and teachers set for children and on children's motivation to work hard to achieve these goals. Effort models offer a more hopeful alternative by providing a simple but constructive formula for ensuring gradual change and improvement. Work hard and persist. (Stevenson and Stigler 1992, 106)

Willingness to Make Mistakes and Coping with Failure

An essential part of learning almost any skill or acquiring virtually any new knowledge is willingness on the part of the learner to make mistakes. As the saying goes, "we learn from our mistakes." Under a cultural model that places primary emphasis on the importance of effort, errors are seen as a natural part of the learning process and therefore viewed by both teachers and learners as positive indicators of accomplishment. Under an ability model, however, errors are more likely to be interpreted as indicators of failure and therefore may serve as signs that the potential (ability) to learn is lacking. Deborah Stipek notes that "children who are concerned about their performance and how smart they look, especially those who also lack confidence, are reluctant to ask for help, even when they need it" (Stipek 2002, 164). As we have noted, therefore, parents who want to encourage their children by telling them how smart they are run the risk of reducing incentives to work hard, take risks, and make mistakes. Similarly, in the classroom, when the primary emphasis is on demonstrating one's ability, students are less likely to ask for assistance than they are when the focus is on learning and understanding.

Whatever one's perspective on the relative importance of ability or effort, learning to cope with failure is essential in order to sustain engagement in most learning situations. All complex learning tasks inevitably involve setbacks and obstacles that must be overcome in order to achieve success. How students respond to these setbacks and failures is a crucial determinant of the outcome of the learning process. Therefore, the capacity to cope with failure is one of the most important capabilities that students must acquire (Alderman 1999; Bandura 1997).

ORGANIZATIONAL EFFECTS OF BELIEFS
ABOUT ABILITY VERSUS EFFORT

A belief in the relative importance of innate abilities can lead naturally to the assumption that children with different abilities should be educated differently in order to maximize their full potential. In the Russell Sage Foundation research on the social effects of standardized testing, for example, a substantial majority of teachers and counselors expressed the view that IQ test scores should be given considerable weight in making important decisions about students, including grouping for instructional purposes (Goslin 1967). Over the last century, educators and parents alike have hotly debated the effects and effectiveness of ability grouping. On one side, there are those who have taken the position that

It Is Okay to Make Mistakes

Work-inhibited students tend to avoid some tasks because they fear failure. They do not realize that failure is normal and necessary for learning. These students need to modify their thinking about schoolwork—that it is okay to make mistakes, that is even beneficial to make errors when developing new skills and knowledge.

Teachers are often poor models for the value of failure. It is not hard to imagine a second-grade student believing the teacher never makes mistakes. Furthermore, teachers reward perfection, not sloppy papers and misspelled words.

Mistakes Are Part of Learning

It is important to *teach* students how to cope with failure. Students may remember their early failures in learning to ride a bike or a skateboard, or learning to swim. Hold class discussions about how mistakes are made while learning new tasks, both in and out of school.

Students may study how famous people learned to cope with and benefit from failure. Discussions may be held about popular movies in which heroes come back from repeated adversity and prevail by not giving up.

Teachers Model Their Own Mistakes

Teachers may be positive models by pointing out their own mistake-making. "I didn't do that correctly." "I made a mistake." "I can't solve this problem. I guess I need more information." "The way I'm doing this is not working. I wonder how I might do it differently?"

Through modeling, teachers can show students that it is okay to try, emphasizing the importance of effort, not perfect papers.

Excerpt from Jerome H. Bruns, *They Can but They Don't* (New York: Penguin Books, 1992), 116.

the same high standards of accomplishment, including the mastery of core academic subjects, can and should be expected of all students and that ability grouping only impedes achievement of this goal. Others have argued that the goal of education should be to provide each student with opportunities to maximize his or her own potential and that separating children according to their abilities makes this possible.

From the mid-1960s to the end of the 1980s, a large number of studies were conducted on the effects of ability grouping in American schools. A review of many of these studies conducted between 1960 and 1974 carried out by Harvard statistician Fred Mosteller (Mosteller, Light, and Sachs 1996) found that if these studies demonstrated any benefit from the practice of ability grouping, it was to the advantage of high-ability students, but the results were not clear (Viadero 1998).[1]

By the mid-1990s, the conventional wisdom among education experts was that the practice of ability grouping was outdated and harmful, especially to those students consigned to lower-ability groups. Notwithstanding this consensus, the practice of separating children in accordance with their abilities, both within classrooms and in centers for the gifted and talented and for those with special educational needs, has continued in American schools, particularly at the elementary and middle school levels. The practice remains popular with parents, especially those of high-achieving students, as well as many teachers, who find it easier to gear their instruction to students of similar ability levels.

More recently, two apparently contradictory developments have occurred. One has been reaffirmation of the principle that all students should be required to meet the same high standards of accomplishment in school. From the beginning of what has become known as "the standards movement" in the early 1990s, through demands for more accountability and rigorous assessments of student performance to the current administration's mantra that "no child shall be left behind," state and local school systems have been under increasing pressure to establish clear standards for what students should know, and to do whatever is necessary to ensure that all students meet these standards. Forty-nine states now have adopted statewide standards in core subjects that students at different grade levels are expected to meet, most states measure student or school performance in meeting these standards, forty-two states participate in the National Assessment of Educational Progress, and forty-three states issue report cards on school performance in relation to the standards (*Education Week* 2002, 74–75).

At the same time, there has been a movement for the reappraisal of policy decisions that led to "detracking" of some students. This reappraisal was stimulated by new studies indicating that while detracking may boost test scores of students in the bottom tracks, these gains come at the expense of average- and high-achieving students, who may be negatively affected. In a sense, these findings reinforce the general conclusion that simply assigning a student to a particular group or track can influence that student's performance, for better or worse, irrespective of the student's abilities, or, indeed, effort (see Stipek 2002, 220).

It seems unlikely that schools are going to be willing to abandon the practice of grouping students by ability any time soon. The growing diversity in the makeup of student populations, moreover, seems certain to result in increased pressure from parents of high-ability students to provide accelerated learning opportunities for their children. Whether schools' responses to such pressures take the form of special programs for gifted and talented students at the elementary and middle school levels, or advanced placement courses at the high school level, the resulting separation of students into groups according to some measures of intellectual ability inevitably has the effect of reinforcing cultural beliefs about inherited differences in ability, as well as directly influencing many students' perceptions of their own abilities.

CONCLUSIONS

One of the most important determinants of an individual's willingness to engage in learning is the expectation that he or she will be successful. This expectation, in turn, is influenced by his or her beliefs about the relative importance of effort as compared with ability, together with an assessment of his or her own abilities. To the extent that an individual believes that innate abilities are an important determinant of success in learning, then the individual's perception of his or her abilities becomes more important. A precondition, therefore, for increasing the engagement of students in learning is ensuring that they believe they can and will succeed if they make the necessary effort. A crucially important determinant of students' beliefs about these matters is the expectations that others—in particular, their parents and teachers—hold for their performance.

Despite the beliefs of most Americans about the importance of hard work for success in life, the educational system in the United States is constructed on an "innate ability paradigm," based on certain "taken-for-granted" assumptions about education. According to John Howard (1995), these include:

1. There is a distribution of intelligence within what is considered the "normal" human population.
2. We can specify how much intelligence is needed to learn particular skills and concepts in school, and to fulfill particular vocational or professional functions in adult life.
3. We can employ standardized tests to measure children's intelligence, and then predict who will be able to master which skills and assume which functions. Ability-group placements, matching intellectual demands of curricula to the intelligence of individual children, are made on the basis of these assessments. (Howard 1995, 86)

The problems generated for many children in American schools by such a system are obvious. To the extent that children are sorted by ability, some are excluded from opportunities to engage in certain kinds of learning altogether, while others may be discouraged from exerting the effort necessary to learn. An emphasis on the importance of innate abilities also has the effect of introducing unnecessary complexity into the processes whereby children formulate estimates of their capacity to learn and thereby their inclination to engage in learning. For the most able students, such an emphasis can have the effect of raising expectations and therefore the costs of failure. This can result in reduced incentives to work hard and decrease the willingness to make mistakes. For less able students, it can add to natural uncertainties about whether they will be able to succeed in any learning task, particularly when the task is advertised in advance as being difficult.

Such a belief system also comes into direct conflict with recent pronouncements that "all children can and should be expected to learn to the same high standards." The standards-based school-reform movement has urged the establishment of a single set of "world-class" standards to which schools "would be held accountable" for getting all their students to achieve at that level (Shanker 1995, 51). Whether or not one believes that it is realistic to expect all or even most students to meet such high standards, setting such a goal could serve an important purpose in shifting attention away from the ability-based model toward an effort-based model. Unless students, parents, and teachers alike can be convinced of the usefulness of an effort-based model, significant progress toward achieving our goal is unlikely. The resulting failure of large numbers of students to achieve at high levels is certain to result in a lowering of the standard. Setting the initial standard lower, however, could reduce expectations for the achievement of many students who have the potential to perform at higher levels than they do at present.

The solution to this dilemma would seem to lie in finding ways to strike a better balance between the current preoccupation with students' abilities and an effort-based model of academic achievement. In principle, there is no reason why the existence of differences among children in their innate intellectual capacities cannot be acknowledged, while at the same time placing greater emphasis on the relationship between hard work and achievement. If differences in inherited abilities matter most at the extremes of the distribution, it is reasonable to suppose that for most people, the amount of effort invested accounts for the lion's share of differences in outcomes.

This conclusion suggests that it is not unrealistic to expect a much larger proportion of students to meet significantly higher standards and to set about figuring out what must be done to make this happen. A crucial first step in the process is to modify both parental and teacher expectations about what students can and should be expected to accomplish. Students in schools in which teachers expect all students to learn achieve at a higher level than students in schools where teachers do not have high expectations for all their students (Stipek 2002). A second key element is to ensure that all parties—students, parents, and teachers—have a clear understanding of what students are expected to achieve. Acknowledging that differences in abilities and interests do exist among students may require increased flexibility in the paths that different students are permitted to take to reach such goals, but should

High Expectations Come First

Pacing the floor, in front of a roomful of educators, Anne Arundel County's new school superintendent, Eric Smith looks like a bookish William Hurt, but he's talking like a fired-up preacher man.

"*All* children can succeed!" he roars as he introduces himself to the county in the middle of May. He is in a windowless room in Annapolis, trying to seduce more than 200 public school staffers with his thundering enthusiasm. "All children can learn!" he cries, "And if you believe all children can learn . . ."

He pauses.

"Close your eyes," he tells his audience softly. "And picture an Advanced Placement classroom." He waits.

"How many of you pictured an Advanced Placement classroom filled with poverty?"

Smith's voice gets louder. "How many of you pictured an Advanced Placement classroom filled with minorities?" He is bellowing. "Filled with children who were previously non-English speakers?"

The room is uncomfortably silent. A few are fidgeting. What he is asking here is: How many of you *truly* believe that all children can learn.

Every successful model for increasing the academic achievement of low-performing students—particularly those from groups that historically have lagged behind students from middle- and upper-income families—depends, first and foremost, on raising expectations on the part of both students and teachers for their performance. Eric Smith and other school superintendents, principals, and individual teachers around the country who have been successful in narrowing the gap between high- and low-achieving students have all begun by setting performance goals that elsewhere would be regarded as unrealistic and then accepting no excuses for failure to achieve them. Students and teachers alike must come to believe that they can learn.

Excerpt from Darragh Johnson, "A Classroom Crusade," *The Washington Post Magazine* (November 10, 2002).

not attenuate expectations for their performance. An important implication of this point is that all students must be given the time and resources they need to achieve these goals. Third, if students are to be required to meet higher standards, they and their parents must be given regular feedback on their progress. This requires the establishment of a credible, fair, and uniform evaluation system that is open to all for inspection.

Finally, as Lauren Resnick points out,

> Hard work and real achievement deserve celebration. And celebration invokes future effort. An education system that actively tries to promote effort will make sure that its schools organize important events highlighting the work students are doing and pointing clearly to achievements that meet the publicly established standards. (Resnick 1995, 58)

Most important, rewards for meeting these standards must not be restricted to the highest performing students, but must celebrate the accomplishments of all those who meet these higher expectations for their performance.

Rewards for engagement in learning are examined in greater detail in chapter 4. It should be noted here, however, that succeeding at something we have set out to accomplish is one of the most powerfully rewarding experiences most of us ever have. In setting standards and raising expectations for student performance, therefore, it is important to ensure that as many students as possible have the experience of living up to the expectations set for them, at least in some areas.

NOTE

1. Only ten of these studies met strict criteria of scientific rigor. Mosteller concluded that "appropriate, large-scale multi-site research studies on skill grouping have not yet been carried out even though the issues have been debated as major public concerns within education for most of this century."

4

REWARDS FOR EFFORT

When one asks the question "What motivates a person to exert the energy necessary to learn something?" one of the first things that comes to mind is the reward(s) the learner expects (consciously or unconsciously) to receive for his or her efforts. Indeed, most major learning theories in psychology begin with the basic fact that human beings—as well as other animals, fish, and insects, too—tend to do things for which they are rewarded, or "reinforced" in psychological parlance. Thus, birds quickly learn where the bird feeder is located, rats learn to navigate a maze that leads to food or water, dogs and lions will learn to do tricks in order to receive rewards, and children will learn to do things for which they receive praise. Animals and humans also learn quickly to avoid things that are unpleasant. Although interesting and important questions remain about the precise mechanisms whereby learning takes place in different situations, there is no doubt that rewards and punishments play a central role in motivation and engagement in learning.

INTRINSIC AND EXTRINSIC REWARDS

Rewards and punishments for engagement in learning come in all sizes and shapes. Some rewards seem to be *intrinsic* to particular learning tasks; such tasks are described as being interesting or fascinating or fun or challenging. In some instances, moreover, a particular learning task can lead to feelings of satisfaction or accomplishment on the part of the learner, which makes engagement in such tasks, in and of itself, a rewarding experience. Other rewards, such as grades in school or praise from a parent or teacher or monetary rewards are unrelated per se, and therefore *extrinsic* to the learning task. Engagement in many learning tasks can generate both intrinsic and extrinsic rewards for the learner. Some rewards, such as praise from a teacher or intrinsic enjoyment, provide immediate gratification to the learner. Others, such as admission to college or employment in a good job, are only distantly related to the learning task.

From the first moments of life, many of the things parents do instinctively to reinforce certain behaviors and to motivate their children to acquire new knowledge and skills are predicated on these characteristics of human beings. The first sounds an infant makes that bear some resemblance to a word are certain to elicit an outpouring of positive responses from his or her parents. Outside the family, rewards and punishments are woven into the fabric of all learning environments, from music lessons to tennis camp to schools and universities. Yet many questions still exist about the way in which rewards and punishments affect motivation for different people in different situations:

- What things constitute rewards for different individuals in different situations? What is the definition of a reward?
- How can one determine what rewards will be most effective in motivating particular individuals to engage in a learning task? To stay engaged?
- What causes something that has been an effective reward to stop serving as a source of motivation for a particular individual?
- How do rewards that are intrinsic to the learning task differ from rewards that are extrinsic to the task? Is one type more effective than the other?
- What is the mechanism that causes some activities to be inherently interesting or enjoyable to some individuals (and perhaps not to others)?

- Under what conditions can rewards have a negative effect on learning and what can be done to avoid such effects?
- What can be done to increase the availability of rewards in schools and other learning environments, including the family?
- What role can or should punishment play in motivating individuals to engage in learning? What negative effects can punishment have, and how can these be avoided?

These questions and many others have been the focus of a great deal of research by psychologists and of attention by educators over the last century. Historically, the issue of the relative effectiveness of intrinsic versus extrinsic rewards for motivation and learning has been at the center of many, if not most, of the great debates in the field of education. Does one begin, for example, with a conception of children as naturally curious about their environments, interested in a wide range of the things with which they come into contact, and motivated to explore the world around them? Or does one view children as, at best, neutral with respect to their interests in their surroundings and their inclination to engage in the process of learning? If the former perspective serves as the guide, then more emphasis should be given to the creation of learning tasks and environments that will be intrinsically interesting and motivating, in and of themselves. Among other things, one will be particularly concerned about making sure that nothing is done to stifle children's natural interests—that is, to turn them off. If, on the other hand, one's inclination is to view children as essentially unmotivated to begin with, more time will be spent thinking about what external tools—rewards and punishments—can be used to motivate children's participation in the learning process.

The reality, of course, is that both perspectives are valid. By now, there is ample evidence to support the view that humans "from birth onwards, in their healthiest states, are active, inquisitive, curious and playful creatures, displaying a ubiquitous readiness to learn and explore and they do not require extraneous incentives to do so" (Ryan and Deci 2000). This conclusion is consistent with the results of experimental studies of animal behavior, which demonstrate that many animals engage naturally in exploratory, playful, and curiosity-driven behavior without reinforcement or reward (White 1959, reported in Ryan and

Deci 2000). These insights about the nature of humans underlie the perspectives of many of the major developmental psychologists and educators, including John Dewey, Jean Piaget, Maria Montessori and, most recently, Howard Gardner (Wagner 2002).

At the same time, behavioral psychologists have been conducting studies of both human and animal learning for most of the last century and there is now a very significant body of experimental evidence that clearly demonstrates the powerful effects of both positive and negative extrinsic reinforcement on motivation and learning. Among the most striking examples of the power of extrinsic rewards to motivate behavior are B. F. Skinner's (1953, 1968) experiments using variable schedules of rewards. He found that by providing rewards (food) to his subjects (pigeons, for example) only some of the time, on a randomly varying schedule, he was able to induce behavior (pecking at a target, for example) that was so persistent that it continued long after he had stopped providing rewards. Skinner's concept of partial, random reinforcement explains the powerful motivation that keeps many gamblers at the table or slot machine even though they win infrequently.

Changing perspectives on the relative importance of intrinsic versus extrinsic rewards has been reflected in major changes that have occurred in education policy and philosophy throughout the last century. John Dewey's beliefs in the child's "natural impulses to conversation, to inquiry, to construction, and to expression," which were seen as natural resources, as "the uninvested capital" of the educative process (Cremin 1961), served in part as the underpinnings of the progressive movement, which exerted profound influence on American education from the early part of the century until after World War II. Among other things, the progressive movement envisioned an education system that was responsive to a wide range of student interests and needs, where the primary role of the teacher was to serve as a guide, and where a major goal of the entire process was the release of a student's creative energies. The focal point of the educational process, therefore, was the interaction between the interests of the student and the subject matter to be conveyed.

More recently, the "back to basics" movement, coupled with a demand for higher standards and accountability, has served to reemphasize the importance of extrinsic rewards and punishments. An increased focus on achievement in a few core subjects, irrespective of student interests and needs, leads to greater reliance on extrinsic rewards and punishments—for example, standardized test scores—for both students and teachers. The remainder of this chapter is devoted to a closer look at these two approaches to motivating students to engage in learning and their implications for educational practice and policy.

INTRINSIC REWARDS AND LEARNING

Intrinsic rewards are those that result from engagement in particular activities, in and of themselves. They are often viewed as somehow residing in specific activities but, in fact, they are generated by interaction between characteristics of the activity and the individual participating in that activity. Participation in a specific activity, therefore, is likely to turn out to be intrinsically rewarding to some individuals and not to others. Some activities—for example, playing games, watching movies, or listening to music—turn out to be pleasurable and therefore intrinsically rewarding activities for most, but not all, of those who participate in them. Other activities—for example, solving mathematical problems or learning to speak a new language—are intrinsically rewarding to some people, but perhaps not to most of those who engage in them, at least at the outset.

Participating in some activities is intrinsically rewarding (enjoyable, interesting, fun) to many people from the moment that they begin to engage in the activity. In other instances, however, it may be necessary for participants in an activity to achieve some level of skill (competence) before the activity becomes intrinsically rewarding. Games requiring at least minimum physical or mental skills, such as golf, tennis, chess, or bridge, are good examples of the latter activities, as is learning to play a musical instrument. Still other activities that initially are uninteresting or unpleasant, or perceived as difficult or dangerous, eventually may become intrinsically engaging for some participants, but the transition from extrinsic to intrinsic rewards is likely to take longer and may be more uncertain.

Understanding the process by which extrinsic rewards come to be replaced by intrinsic rewards as a result of engagement in any particular activity and the variables that influence this transition are of enormous potential importance in education. Equally important is a better understanding of what makes some activities intrinsically interesting and therefore rewarding to some people and not to others. Ryan and Deci (2000) assert, for example, that:

> Despite the observable evidence that humans are liberally endowed with intrinsic motivational tendencies, this propensity appears to be expressed only under specifiable conditions. Research into intrinsic motivation has thus placed much emphasis on those conditions that elicit, sustain, and enhance this special type of motivation versus those that subdue or diminish it. . . . This language reflects the assumption that intrinsic motivation, being an inherent organismic propensity, is catalyzed (rather than caused) when individuals are in conditions that are conducive to its expression. (58)

In conceptualizing these issues, Ryan and Deci (2000) start from the theoretical assumption that, in addition to the inclination to engage in activities that are inherently interesting, humans possess innate psychological needs for competence and autonomy. From this platform, they argue that "interpersonal events and structures (e.g., rewards, communications, feedback) that [lead to] feelings of competence during action can enhance intrinsic motivation . . . because they satisfy the basic psychological need for competence." It is hard to imagine tennis, chess, playing the piano, or reading generating intrinsic rewards and therefore engaging the energies of someone who is unable to achieve even a minimal level of competence in these activities. They hypothesize, further, that feelings of competence will not enhance intrinsic motivation unless they are accompanied by a perceived sense of autonomy—that is, a sense on the part of the individual that he or she is in control of the situation. An important implication of the latter hypothesis is that the introduction of extrinsic rewards for performance in an activity that had heretofore been generating intrinsic rewards can undermine the participant's intrinsic motivation by reducing his perceived sense of control. Numerous experimental studies provide support for the foregoing hypotheses. The authors conclude that "classroom and home environments can facilitate or forestall intrinsic motivation by supporting versus thwarting the needs for autonomy and competence" (59).

The foregoing notions suggest that sustaining the motivation to participate in an activity in which the rewards are primarily intrinsic as opposed to extrinsic to the activity depends importantly on whether the participant gains a sense of competence in his or her performance. Initially, a sense of competence may be generated simply by evidence that one is making progress in acquiring the necessary skills. If, however, one encounters difficulties, or finds that he or she is not continuing to progress, his or her sense of competence may suffer. The result is diminution of intrinsic rewards, irrespective of how interesting or enjoyable the activity might have been at the outset. At this point, extrinsic rewards of one sort or another may be necessary to sustain the learner's level of motivation and participation in the activity until a sense of competence and self-efficacy, and with it the possibility of intrinsic rewards, is restored.

Looking at the process this way suggests that sustaining participation in most learning tasks and especially those that are complex and difficult requires a constantly changing mixture of rewards that are intrinsic and extrinsic to the activity. Thus, for example, a prospective learner might easily be motivated to learn how to play the piano because of the intrinsically pleasurable sounds that it is possible to make at the beginning. Except in rare cases, however, extrinsic rewards (and possibly the threats of punishment) will be necessary to sustain this motivation over time as the learner encounters difficulties that threaten his or her perception of competence and therefore diminish the intrinsic rewards. If the learner perseveres, feelings of competence are likely to be restored, along with the intrinsic pleasures associated with the music that one is able to make. At this point, intrinsic rewards may once again serve as the primary source of the learner's motivation.

It seems likely that good teachers understand at some level the interplay between intrinsic and extrinsic rewards in generating and sustaining the engagement of their pupils in learning. Teachers seek to arouse the interest of their students in the subject they are teaching, thus offering the possibility that intrinsic rewards will follow from their students' participation and engagement ("You are really going to like this book," "You will discover that this is a fascinating problem to work on," etc.). At the same time, they may offer extrinsic rewards if students take the first steps toward engagement, and they are ready to bolster students' feelings of competence with praise for their performance at the first sign of progress in acquiring the desired knowledge or skill. In attempting to find the right balance between reliance on extrinsic versus intrinsic rewards, good teachers are sensitive to the students' needs for feelings of both competence and at least some measure of autonomy if intrinsic rewards are to play a significant part in the student's motivation over time.

There are several reasons for the special interest that intrinsic rewards generate in education. First, if ways can be found of making learning tasks intrinsically rewarding to students, then presumably less time and energy will need to be devoted to providing extrinsic rewards in order to keep students engaged in the learning process. With sufficient intrinsic rewards being generated by the activity itself, students will continue to exert the effort necessary to learn, which in turn will generate more intrinsic rewards, and so on. All that teachers will need to do is provide the content. They can become the "guides" idealized by the progressive movement in education. Second, there is ample evidence that when students reach some threshold level of competence, at least for some activities, intrinsic rewards become so powerful that the machine essentially will run forever unless something unusual happens to turn it off. Becoming an expert in some activity, be it mathematics, science, chess, playing the piano, tennis, golf, or skateboarding, turns out to be remarkably motivating. Finally, there is some evidence that the pursuit of rewards that are intrinsic to a learning task, in contrast to extrinsic rewards, can result in "higher-quality learning" and more creativity on the part of the learner. External rewards also can distract learners from a focus on the learning task and, in extreme cases, engender resentment, resistance, and disinterest on the part of learners (Ryan and Deci 2000, 55). It may not be an overstatement to say that every teacher's goal is to make every learning task intrinsically rewarding to his or her students, however fanciful this goal may be.

What Makes Something Intrinsically Rewarding?

When one thinks of things that most people naturally enjoy doing, what comes to mind first are games (including spectator sports), aesthetic activities (art, music, and drama), and experiences that challenge us or excite our senses (exploring a new place, roller coasters, exercise, scuba diving, hunting, and fishing). Intrinsically rewarding activities appeal to humans' natural curiosity, playfulness, and desire for stimulation. Intuitively, this makes sense, as does the foregoing list of things that most people would put in a category of likely-to-be intrinsically rewarding activities. In a word, they are all things that at least some people would describe as "fun."

The problem is that everything in this category of activities is not equally appealing (i.e., intrinsically rewarding) to everyone. Even within this list of apparently pleasurable activities, what one person finds to be intrinsically rewarding may not appeal to someone else. Some people love to ride on roller coasters; others are frightened by the thought of riding on one. Some individuals enjoy playing bridge, others gravitate to chess, gin rummy, or poker. Some people like competitive team sports; others prefer to run or lift weights on their own. Some love going to the theater or to the movies; others would rather go fishing or hunting. Some people enjoy participating in many different activities; others find only a few to be intrinsically rewarding. These commonsense observations lead to the conclusion that characteristics of a person help to determine what activities are likely to be intrinsically rewarding, especially at the outset; to paraphrase an old Quaker adage, some activities "speak to the condition" of some people, as opposed to others.

There is very little systematic information on the origins of individual predispositions to engage in, and to find intrinsically rewarding, different activities. It may be assumed that genetic factors play some role in such predispositions as they do in almost all human characteristics and their behaviors. Similarly, it is clear that experiences beginning in early childhood affect the kinds of things different individuals find intrinsically rewarding. Disentangling these influences, however, thus far has proved to be elusive. It is well known, for example, that children who demonstrate great interest in and talent for music at a very early age are not only much more likely to have parents who are musicians but also to have grown up in families in which they have been surrounded by music from the beginning. The extent to which these predispositions are the result of genetic as opposed to experiential factors is as yet unknown.

An interesting set of perspectives on the source of predispositions to find one activity versus another intrinsically rewarding is generated by the work of Omar K. Moore on the role of what he calls "autotelic folk models" in both socialization and education. Moore and his colleague Alan Ross Anderson (1969) postulate that every culture incorporates a variety of special activities that play a vitally important role in helping members of the society learn how to deal with the major problems they are likely to encounter in the course of their lives. These activities have several important characteristics. They are (1) intrinsically interesting to members of society (so that people will be inclined to engage in them— hence the term *autotelic*, or containing their own source of motivation); (2) protected from penalties for serious mistakes (so that participants can try out different solutions to the problems presented without suffering serious consequences); and (3) accurate representations of real, serious problems with which members of society eventually must deal. Moore and Anderson identify four classes of such activities: *puzzles*, which enable participants to explore their physical environment and to develop a sense of control over elements of that environment; *games of chance*, which enable participants to learn about and deal with events over which they have no control; *games of strategy*, which enables participants to learn how to take the role of others in dealing with those around them; and *aesthetic activities*, which enable participants to explore their emotions, as well as a wide range of normative and judgmental behaviors.

It is easy to see that almost any example of a potentially intrinsically rewarding (i.e., interesting, enjoyable, fun) activity one can think of can be placed in one or another (and often more than one) of these classes of activities, from playing on a playground jungle gym to watching an opera. Thus, for example, both poker and bridge require participants to take account of probabilities that events beyond their control will or will not occur, as well as understanding the behavior of others, while chess depends solely on predicting or responding to the behavior of one's opponent. Moore and Anderson's theory contributes to the notion that these inherently enjoyable and therefore intrinsically rewarding activities also play an essential role in preparing members of the society to deal with more important problems and events they are likely to encounter in the course of their lives. From this insight, it is only a short step to the hypothesis that individuals gravitate naturally toward those activities that also help them learn to deal with the most significant problems in their lives. To repeat the Quaker phrase: these activities "speak to the condition" of those who find them especially rewarding.

The preconceptions individuals bring to any particular learning task also have much to do with whether the activity turns out to be intrinsically rewarding. These preconceptions are shaped by a number of influences, including how the activity is introduced to them by others, whether they discover it on their own, and what they might have been told or learned about the activity in advance. Infants and very young children approach most learning tasks with few, if any, preconceptions about whether they will enjoy it or how difficult it might be. In part, for this reason, children accomplish one of the most difficult learning tasks that they will encounter at any time in their lives—learning to talk— with remarkable speed and apparently without undue effort. Similarly, there is ample evidence that the acquisition of a second language is easier the earlier it is attempted. By the time children enter school, however, they approach most new learning tasks with a set of preconceptions that have been shaped by parents, teachers, older siblings, peers, and others. Initial views of even those things that most people regard as intrinsically rewarding are strongly influenced by what they may have learned about the activity in advance, as well as the immediate context in which it is encountered.

These factors affect the initial choices people make about a wide range of recreational activities. In an educational context, what students may have learned about a particular learning task in advance or the way it is presented to them by teachers can have a significant impact on the likelihood that engagement in the activity will turn out to be intrinsically rewarding. If students approach a subject in school with the expectation that it will turn out to be interesting or enjoyable, they are more likely to perceive it as interesting and enjoyable. Conversely, subjects that students are led to think of as boring, difficult, or irrelevant are less likely to generate intrinsic rewards, at least at the outset.

An example of the potential effect of such influences on student engagement in learning is provided by a comparison of cultural beliefs about the teaching of mathematics in Japan and the United States. In their comparative study of teaching practices in several cultures, including the United States, Japan, and Germany, James Stigler and James Hiebert (1999) found that mathematics teachers in the United States tended to view their subject as primarily a set of procedures for solving problems. Almost two-thirds of U.S. mathematics teachers reported that the "main thing" they wanted students to learn from their lessons were methods and skills needed to solve various kinds of problems. Moreover, U.S. teachers "also seem to believe that learning terms and practicing skills is not very exciting" (89). In accordance with these beliefs, mathematics teachers in U.S. schools tended to employ a variety of instructional techniques that rely heavily on extrinsic rewards to motivate students.

In contrast, "Japanese teachers act as if mathematics is inherently interesting and students will be interested in exploring it by developing new methods for solving problems. They seem less concerned about motivating the topics in nonmathematical ways" (90). This assumption manifests itself in teaching methods that present mathematics as a set of relationships among concepts, facts, and procedures. These relationships are revealed by "developing solution methods to problems, studying the methods, working toward increasingly efficient methods, and talking explicitly about the relationships of interest" (89). Japanese teachers responded to the question about the main thing they wanted their students to learn from the lessons by saying that they wanted their students to think about things in a new way, such as to see new relationships between mathematical ideas (see "A Fifth-Grade Mathematics Lesson in Japan" in chapter 5).

The foregoing beliefs about mathematics are reflected in important differences in the way mathematics is taught in Japan and the United States. In this country, the methods reinforce stereotypical views of American children about mathematics as being tedious and uninteresting. Viewing mathematics as a set of procedures leads to a curriculum organized around mastering these procedures one by one, relying on extensive practice at each stage to ensure that the student has command of each procedure before proceeding to the next state of difficulty. Most American parents will recognize this method in the worksheets and exercises that typically comprise their children's homework. In contrast, Japanese teachers are more likely to begin by allowing students to struggle with problems, trying out different solutions, and then discussing which methods seem to work best and why. It does not seem surprising that most American students do not regard learning mathematics as an intrinsically interesting activity.

Why Things Stop Being Intrinsically Rewarding

Most people are familiar with the experience of losing interest in an activity that for some period of time had been highly engaging. Teenagers who for a time appear to be addicted to a particular computer game, for example, suddenly find that it is no longer rewarding. This abandonment of previously highly motivating activities often occurs after a participant has become extremely competent; indeed, so competent that the activity no longer offers any new challenge. The notion that an activity must continue to present a challenge in order to sustain an individual's interest represents an important addition to the list of attributes that help to make something intrinsically rewarding. It also requires modification of assumptions about the importance of competence alone as a mediator of intrinsic rewards. Being able to do something well, by itself, may not be enough to ensure that the activity will continue to engage an individual's interest over time.

The idea that intrinsically rewarding activities include an element of challenge is consistent with the basic conceptual framework that relates intrinsic rewards to satisfaction of humans' innate curiosity and interest in exploring the unknown. Inherent in the notion of a challenge is uncertainty about the outcome of the activity. When one reaches the point where there is no longer a question about how something will turn out (e.g., one is certain that he can beat the computer game), then the challenge disappears and with it the capacity of the activity to continue to generate intrinsic rewards. The principle of uncertainty of outcome helps to explain why some activities seem never to lose their capacity to generate intrinsic rewards for those who participate in them—for example, games and other activities involving an element of chance, as well as those that are contingent on the behavior of others (which typically contain an element of unpredictability). Moreover, it may be hypothesized that the more complex the activity—that is, the more variables that must be taken into account in order to predict accurately the outcome—the more intrinsically rewarding the activity will turn out to be. It comes as no surprise, therefore, that chess, bridge, poker, fishing and hunting, golf and tennis, sailboat racing, and all major team sports, not to mention literature, science, and mathematics, turn out to be as intrinsically engaging as they are. The complexity principle may also help to explain why classical music and drama continue to engage so many people.

Intrinsic Motivation and the "Professionalization" of Children's Sports

Before the early 1970s, most of the games children played after school and during the summer were organized by children themselves. Kids played baseball, basketball, football, and many other games, in the appropriate season, in school yards, playgrounds, and in neighborhood streets, typically without intervention or supervision from adults. Participants took responsibility for organizing the games, establishing the rules, and enforcing them. In so doing, children learned many things in addition to the skills necessary to play the sport, including leadership, organizational and negotiating skills, as well as the importance of playing by the rules. More important from a motivational perspective, such activities met the essential condition of giving participants a sense of control over the situation and their participation in it. (Kids really could threaten to take their ball and go home, or quit and leave the team without enough players.) Finally, while the games often were no less competitive than they are today, the absence of adults, especially parents, enabled players to develop their skills and make mistakes without suffering serious (in their eyes) consequences.

Beginning in the 1970s, adults essentially took over children's sports. First with Little League baseball and eventually expanding to basketball, football and, more recently soccer (and even lacrosse!), the vast majority of children's games now are formally organized and supervised by adults. Few children have time or the opportunity to organize informal games; nor for the most part can they decide about what activities they will participate in or when they will play. Decisions about what positions they will play on the team are made by coaches, as are the strategies to be employed in the course of the game. The result is that players have little, if any, autonomy or sense of control. As children's sports have become more organized, they have also come to have more serious consequences in the lives of participants. Parents coach, attend games, and cheer for their children. Success and failure, not only in the eyes of teammates but also in the eyes of their parents, have become part of the game. We must ask whether one of the most important classes of socializing activities has been seriously degraded, if not lost altogether.

In conclusion, the major reason why some activities cease to be intrinsically rewarding is that external events and forces change either participants or the activity in such a way as to (1) diminish or eliminate the intrinsic rewards participants are receiving or (2) introduce competing extrinsic rewards or punishments for the same or some other activity. It is not possible or necessary to enumerate all of the circumstances that fall under these two headings. Suffice it to say that in the first instance they include a wide range of things from changes in the capabilities of participants to changes in characteristics of the activity. In the context of school, modifications to teaching methods introduced by a new teacher, as a result of a new curriculum, or as a result of a new assessment system could have such effects. In the second instance, the introduction of extrinsic rewards, accompanied by loss of autonomy for participants, into activities that had been primarily intrinsically motivating (for example, Little League baseball, in contrast to school-yard games) can diminish the salience of intrinsic rewards. Finally, as we see in the next section of this chapter and again in chapter 6, activities that generate intrinsic rewards must compete for children's attention with many other activities and sources of rewards, many of them external to learning tasks.

EXTRINSIC REWARDS AND LEARNING

Extrinsic rewards are conceptually separable from the specific activities involved in learning a particular skill or acquiring knowledge. As discussed above, a number of different things can serve as extrinsic rewards for engagement in learning, including:

- *Interpersonal rewards.* Perhaps the most powerful class of external rewards involves interactions between the learner and significant others, including parents, other family members, teachers, and peers, who have important relationships to the learner. Such rewards include various forms of praise, attention, encouragement, positive judgments about the learner's performance, and other expressions of support.
- *Feedback on performance.* Another category includes more formal performance ratings, such as grades in school or test scores, or the

awards for competition in school, on the athletic field, or in some other arena. Both this and the foregoing category of rewards are especially important because they relate more or less directly to specific learning tasks and activities.

- *Market incentives.* Almost anything that has tangible value to the student can serve as a reward for engagement in a learning task, including money or prizes, being excused from a homework assignment, going to the movies or the school dance, or any other special privileges within the family or school.
- *Goal-based rewards.* The achievement of short- or long-term goals—getting a good grade in mathematics, making the honor roll, achieving a high grade point average, graduating from high school, gaining admission to college, or obtaining a good job—set by or for the learner can and do function as extrinsic rewards.
- *Avoidance of punishment.* One way of thinking about the role of punishment in motivation is that the avoidance of punishment can have the effect of a positive reward. Credible threats of punishment by parents or teachers, therefore, can serve to motivate students to engage in learning tasks, doing their homework, or practicing the piano.

These extrinsic rewards obviously vary in their relevance to the learning task, as well as their proximity in time to the specific behaviors for which they serve as a reward. Praise from a teacher for paying attention in class or answering a question correctly, or from a parent for completing one's homework are rewards that are both related to the task and closely connected in time to the specific activities they are intended to motivate. Research suggests that this is one of the reasons for their power to motivate behavior on the part of students. Test scores and grades in school also are related to learning tasks, but are usually somewhat more distant in time from the behaviors they are intended to reinforce. The frequency with which they are used and their perceived relevance to learning tasks, however, makes them especially salient for many students. Long-term goals such as graduation from high school, getting into college, getting a job, or earning a good living, vary greatly in the degree to which they are seen as related to current learning tasks. While they serve as important potential extrinsic rewards for many students, for others they are perceived as remote or, worse, irrelevant. Their power to stimulate and sustain motivation and engagement in learning, therefore, varies greatly from student to student.

As was the case with intrinsic rewards, the power of a particular potential external reward to motivate action on the part of any given individual depends as much upon the characteristics and state of the individual as on the type of reward. Things that are highly rewarding and therefore motivating for one person may have little or no meaning for or effect on someone else. At the same time, everyone has some intuitive sense of the kinds of things that are rewarding to most people, most of the time. Underlying this intuition is the notion that people share many of the same needs, desires, and goals. Things that satisfy these needs, desires, and goals have the capacity to serve as external rewards.

Interpersonal Rewards

Extrinsic rewards that result from the learner's relationship with other people depend both on the learner's needs and desires, and on the nature of the relationship with those whose behavior has the potential to be rewarding. Most individuals have close relationships with a set of significant others whose praise, encouragement, and judgments about the learner's performance have an especially strong potential to reward (or punish) the learner's behavior and therefore to influence his or her motivation. For most people, these significant others include parents and other close relatives, at least some teachers, and peers. Any person with whom an individual comes into contact can deliver rewards (and punishments), but significant others have the greatest potential to influence behavior because of the importance of their relationship to the person. It is for this reason that parental encouragement and rewards for their children's engagement in learning are of such critical importance to their success in school.

Praise is by far the most common extrinsic reward used in all educational settings (Stipek 2002). There is good evidence that praise can and does serve as a positive reinforcement for engagement in learning, especially for young children. Like all extrinsic rewards, however, it can be ineffective or have negative effects under some circumstances. To be effective, for example, praise must be contingent upon the behavior one wishes to maintain or increase, such as exerting effort, and it must be credible in the eyes of the learner. Stipek also makes the important point that praise can be used as an integral part of the instructional process itself, to inform students of what the teacher expects from his or her students and to focus attention on particular aspects of their performance.

Formal Reward Systems

All educational institutions incorporate a variety of more or less formal systems for providing feedback to students about their performance. In most schools, students receive periodic formal appraisals of their progress in learning, which often include judgments about how much effort they are investing in learning. In addition, students are likely to receive frequent feedback in the form of scores on tests created and administered by their teachers. Finally, virtually all school systems now make regular use of a variety of standardized tests to assess student performance; in most cases, the results of these tests are reported to parents. Obviously, the feedback that children and their parents receive from these formal reporting systems is more rewarding and therefore potentially motivating to some children and parents than to others.

This leads to an important dilemma for teachers and schools. If all children were to receive good grades for their performance when, in fact, some students perform better than others, it is widely assumed that the value of grades as rewards would be diminished. On the other hand, if only some children receive high grades, grades serve only to motivate these successful students and not others. Teachers and schools have attempted to find ways to resolve this dilemma for generations, but it remains one of the most perplexing issues that schools must address.

In addition to grades and test scores, schools and other institutions that offer organized learning activities for children (for example, Odyssey of the Mind, Future Problem Solvers, science fairs, extracurricular activity clubs in schools, athletic programs, camps) have established a variety of other mechanisms for recognizing and rewarding the achievements of children. Honor rolls, special scholastic awards, and awards for academic and nonacademic competition both in school and out, generate a regular flow of rewards for many students. These rewards, however, are accessible only to students who participate in such activities or who excel in their academic work.

Privileges and Threats of Punishment

Every parent makes frequent use of threats of punishment or promises of extrinsic rewards to motivate their children to do household chores, clean their room, do homework, or practice a musical instrument. As noted above, almost anything that is perceived by the child as valuable can serve as a reward for particular desired behaviors, including the expenditure of effort and engagement in learning. The range of things that meet this condition (i.e., being valuable to a child) is very wide, from money (allowances, opportunities to earn extra money for work around the house, etc.) to participation in family activities to special privileges (being allowed to watch TV, stay up late, etc.). Threats to withhold things that children value can be and frequently are used in a similar fashion to motivate desired behaviors. In school, many teachers also make use of the promise of extrinsic rewards (or threats to withhold them) to motivate their students to pay attention in class, work harder, or behave well. Some schools have experimented with elaborate systems of market-type rewards for student performance, such as payment of tokens that can be redeemed for various privileges or even tangible goods such as candy or ice cream (Stipek 2002, 23–24).

Such rewards clearly can be useful in motivating students to engage in learning, but they have several important potential negative consequences. First, when students do things because they expect to receive some reward that is completely unrelated to whatever it is they are asked to do, they may tend to focus more on getting the reward than on the task at hand. Reliance on such rewards over time as a primary mechanism for motivating students to engage in learning, therefore, runs the risk of distracting students' attention away from the learning task, to the detriment of any learning that might occur. The more valuable the reward is perceived to be, the more distracting it is likely to be. Second, under such conditions, students are likely to do only as much as it takes to obtain the promised reward and no more. Studies have shown, for example, that extrinsic rewards can have a negative effect on children's willingness to tackle difficult problems, and can lead to superficial learning behaviors, less flexible problem-solving strategies, and less creativity (Stipek 2002, 28). Third, these effects of extrinsic rewards can reduce the likelihood that students will become engaged in the learning task itself and therefore be less motivated to continue to exert effort when the extrinsic rewards end. Finally, as will be discussed in chapter 7, deals that parents and teachers enter into with their children involving the exchange of extrinsic rewards for particular behaviors can have a variety of negative effects on the learning environment.

Individual Goals

A central focus of attention among scientists who study motivation is the role played by an individual's goals in motivating his or her behavior (Pintrich 2000; Zimmerman 2000; Wentzel 2000; Bandura 1977, 1997). A great deal of evidence exists that individuals set a wide variety of goals for themselves, that they exert varying amounts of effort to achieve these goals, and that perceived progress toward achieving these goals is rewarding and therefore motivating to the individual (Wentzel 2000). Individual goals may be short or long term with regard to when they might be achieved, and either highly task specific or more general in character. Goals also may vary according to how much they are under the conscious control of the individual (i.e., individuals may be more or less aware of the goals toward which they may be striving). It is clear that students set goals for themselves as well as adopt (accept) goals set for them by parents, teachers, and others. Successfully completing high school and being accepted into college, for example, are among the most common long-range goals held by many students. These goals, in turn, are often related to longer-range life and career goals of earning a good living, being able to support a family, increasing one's social status, attaining wealth, and the like. In the short range, these goals are supported by specific task-related goals, such as mastering a particular subject matter, or more general cognitive goals, such as developing one's ability to think creatively (Wentzel 2000). In addition, students may set a variety of other goals, such as gaining approval from others, establishing personal relationships with teachers or peers, cooperating with classmates, or developing inter-personal skills (Wentzel 2000).

Because individual goals are heavily influenced by significant others, as well as by broader social and cultural factors, each individual has a unique and continually changing set of both short- and long-term goals. Assumptions, therefore, about what goals will or should be potentially motivating for any particular individual may or may not be accurate. For example, gaining admission to college may not have any salience for poor children or those from minority groups who do not see this as a re-alistic goal for themselves. Moreover, the potential of rewards for ac-complishment of even short-term academic achievement goals may be perceived as very low by many children and by their families. In such in-stances, the child or his parents may set alternative goals—for example, becoming a good athlete, making money, or having a child—that will become the focus of most of the child's effort.

Self-efficacy and Goals

In the same way that the perception of competence and autonomy are viewed as being essential to the effectiveness of intrinsic rewards, "self-efficacy" has been postulated to be "a potent mediator of students' learn-ing and motivation to achieve one's goals" (Zimmerman 2000). Perceived self-efficacy has been defined as "personal judgments of one's capabilities to organize and execute courses of action to attain designated goals" (Zim-merman 2000; Bandura 1977, 1997). An important aspect of this definition is that feelings of self-efficacy derived from one's perceived capability to perform in a specific task context, as opposed to judgments about personal qualities, including ability. Self-efficacy beliefs are therefore multidimen-sional and dependent upon the task at hand. There is evidence that "self-efficacious students participate more readily, work harder, persist longer and have fewer adverse emotional reactions when they encounter difficul-ties than do those who doubt their capabilities" (Zimmerman 2000, 86). Self-efficacy differs from competence in that it is less closely connected to a specific skill or ability; indeed, it may be regarded as generalized confi-dence in one's capacity to acquire specific skills.

The relevance of self-efficacy beliefs for student motivation and en-gagement in learning has important implications for what is expected of students and the kinds of feedback they receive on their performance. Students' beliefs in their own capabilities can only be developed by enabling them to tackle challenging tasks, as well as to succeed. In his new book *Making the Grade*, Tony Wagner (2002) argues forcefully that requiring students to master real competencies and providing meaningful performance-based assessments of their progress is essential if we are to motivate "students to take on more challenging work and, ultimately, to achieve greater levels of academic competence" (87).

The connection between extrinsic rewards and individual goals suggests that individuals must be aware of their goals in order for a prospective reward to be effective in motivating behavior. This is almost certainly the case when achievement of the goal is widely separated in time from many of the activities that are required to achieve it (e.g., admission to college as the reward for hard work in high school).

EXTRINSIC REWARDS AND SCHOOLS

It is clear that extrinsic rewards play a critically important role in motivating children to engage in learning tasks and to persevere in the face of uninteresting subject matter, difficulty, distractions, and the appeal of other more attractive (intrinsically rewarding) activities. In particular, the crucial role of significant others has been emphasized, not only in encouraging and sustaining effort on the part of students but also in helping them to set goals that, in turn, serve as sources of additional rewards. In addition, the importance of meaningful feedback to students on their performance has been noted. In this context, therefore, the issue of whether an adequate supply of rewards is available to motivate all of the children in our schools must be addressed. In doing so, three major problems become apparent: (a) the increasing scarcity of significant others (in particular, adults) in the lives of children, (b) the factors that prevent schools from providing extrinsic rewards to more than a relatively small fraction of their students on a consistent basis, and (c) the inability of teachers and schools to provide meaningful feedback to many students.

The Scarcity of Significant Others in the Lives of Children

First, a number of observers have called attention to the fact that children in America are growing up increasingly isolated from adults and from the positive relationships with older people that are an important part of everyone's socialization and learning. In addition to the important lessons about life that young people learn from interactions with their parents, members of their extended family, and other adults in the community with whom they develop important relationships (see chapter 6), these significant others are a primary source of rewards for engagement in learning. Over the last four decades, a variety of changes have occurred in our society that have significantly reduced the opportunities most children have for interaction with adults, including members of their own families. The statistics are familiar to us all: more marriages ending in divorce, many more single-parent and dual-career families, fewer members of extended families living under the same roof, more elderly persons living in senior citizen homes and communities, adults working longer hours, and more families living in suburbia where one is required to drive both to work and to obtain almost every other necessity. All of these changes have reduced the opportunities that children and young people have to develop relationships with individuals who can be sources of rewards for engagement in learning.

In addition to the decrease in the number of important adults in children's lives, there is evidence that many American parents take the view that once children reach school age, it is the school's responsibility not only to educate them but also to supervise many other aspects of their lives. Once children reach school age, American parents tend to be less involved in the education of their children than parents in other countries, for example, China and Japan, where a high proportion of parents work closely with their children's teachers and play a strongly supportive role.

The Supply of Extrinsic Rewards in Schools

Just as there has been a profound transformation in family life in this country, there has been a steady increase in the size and complexity of American schools over the last several decades. As a result of demands for greater efficiency, better facilities, and requests for more services and variety in the curriculum, many high schools now enroll more than 3,000 students, with middle and elementary schools also proportionately larger. Typical class sizes have also remained large (despite notable experiments like California's recent class-size reduction initiative) and teaching loads heavy. Although middle and high school students typically have a half dozen or more different teachers, each of these teachers, in turn, must try to keep track of as many as 150 or more students. What are the chances that any of these teachers will be able to pay any real, sustained attention to more than a handful of their students, even on a sporadic basis?

Even more important, most of our schools still operate on what is essentially a scarce reward system. The best and most diligent students receive most of the very good grades, along with the lion's share of the special awards that the school has to offer. The majority of students receive grades that are neither particularly rewarding nor punishing and which therefore do little to affect their motivation to participate actively in the learning process. Students at the lower end of the spectrum receive grades that can only be described as discouraging.

Types of Rewards

The inability of our schools to provide students with useful appraisals of their competencies on many of the skills that are most important for work and citizenship is well known. Psychometricians have been struggling with the task of developing reliable, valid, and affordable measures of relevant and meaningful skills for a long time. By far, the most ambitious effort to date to develop both internationally benchmarked standards for student performance in the major academic subjects as well as an assessment system that would measure student performance against those standards, is the New Standards Project. A joint project of the National Center on Education and the Economy (1996) and the Learning Research and Development Center at the University of Pittsburgh, New Standards released a comprehensive set of performance standards in mathematics, English language arts, science, and applied learning at the elementary, middle, and high school levels in 1996, along with a per-

School Climate

"OK, who's next?"

It's David Smith's humanities class at Central Park East (in New York City) on a Tuesday morning in December. The task is an oral recitation of e. e. cummings's poem "in Just." Kareem, a tall, lanky thirteen-year-old black youth, has just finished a performance that brought down the house. Having watched him regale the class with his interpretation, as he strode around the room, pantomiming the characters, one is hard-pressed to believe David's later claim that this is virtually the first time Kareem has contributed to the class. But then knowing this, the excitement of his peers seems all the more real. Several students get through adequate, but not nearly as theatrical renditions. Others pass, choosing to recite another day. We move around the room, coming to a quiet, reluctant face locked in concentration on his desktop in the hope that he will not be noticed.

"Hua," David asks, "would you like to try?"

The shy southeast Asian youth shakes his head no, still avoiding David's eyes.

"He's new, he's only been here a couple of weeks," I'm informed in hushed tones by the young woman sitting to my left.

"Are you sure?" David tries again, but Hua, obviously a bit ill at ease, doesn't look up. "Well, try this with me. Go get your copy of the poem . . . now read it out loud, don't worry about it, just try; we're here to help you."

Hua hesitates, and he looks around the room. It's as if he is trying to gauge us all, to see if we are to be trusted. He clears his throat, throws one more protesting look at David and prepares to begin.

Before he starts, the young man on my right leans over to me and instructs, "Look, he doesn't speak English real well, so you need to pay attention, listen closely, and don't make fun. OK?" I nod, wondering where his savvy comes from. It's silent in here now; for some reason even the noise of the commuter trains outside can't penetrate the room.

Continued

"in Just —
spring," Hua begins, cautiously, quietly.
"when the world is," he falters, stuck on a cummings-invented word.
"mudluscious," coaches David, softly.
"mudluscious the little
lame balloonman
whistles far and wee
and…" he falters again.
"eddieandbill." This time from a fellow student, whispered as encouragement, not bellowed as one-upmanship.

Hua pushes on with these and other whispered aids. And as he does
the room is almost thick with a sense of triumph. Every member of the
class is on the edge of his or her chair, silently cheering Hua on, hang-
ing on his every word, nodding encouragement, struggling with him on
each difficult pronunciation. None of this is lost on Hua. He picks up
confidence with each line, until even he is smiling as he brings the
verse home.

> "it's
> spring
> and
>   the
>   goat-footed
> balloonman whistles
> far
> and
> wee"

There is silence as we all realize what a moment of personal history this
is for Hua. It is, literally, the first English he has spoken to more than one
person since arriving in the United States. Then sensing it is their history,
their victory as well, cheers and shouts of congratulations fill the room as
Hua grins shyly at his friends and then hides his face.

David, visibly moved (as am I, busily trying to hide tears of emotion behind my field notebook), first thanks Hua, then addresses everyone.

"I think this group can do anything it wants to if it puts its mind to it. And I want to thank you for being so supportive of your new classmate. . . . You are a real family. Thanks."

Excerpt from George H. Wood, *Schools That Work* (New York: Penguin Books, Plume, 1992), 83–85. Reprinted with permission of the publisher.

formance assessment system linked to the standards in mathematics and English. The performance assessment system includes a mix of traditional test items and performance tasks that ask students to use their knowledge to solve complex problems. Performance assessments in science and applied learning are under development.

Despite the significant progress achieved by this and other projects to date, formidable challenges remain. Chief among these is the task of creating both standards for student performance and an accompanying assessment system that capture the diversity and complexity of the skills involved in high-level achievement in any field and, at the same time, can serve as the basis for instruction and assessment on a large scale at reasonable cost. Expanding the range of skills to be measured beyond traditional academic fields—for example, to things such as the ability to work in teams or to generate creative solutions to problems—presents even greater challenges.

Taken together, the foregoing problems suggest that, for the majority of American students, particularly at the middle and high school levels, meaningful extrinsic rewards of any sort for engagement in learning are hard to come by. It should not come as a surprise, therefore, to discover that most students are, at best, only sporadically engaged in learning.

CONCLUSIONS

Both intrinsic and extrinsic rewards clearly play a crucial role in the process of initiating and sustaining a learner's engagement in learning. Few, if any, learning tasks are engaging enough, in and of themselves, to sustain the motivation of all or even most prospective learners over time.

Moreover, even the most interesting and engaging learning tasks are unlikely to be intrinsically engaging to all learners. At the same time, reliance solely on extrinsic rewards, even if such rewards were readily available, is both costly and inefficient, and almost certainly would have a negative effect on the learning process itself.

The compelling image that emerges from this analysis is that sustained engagement in the learning process depends upon a continuous interplay among intrinsic and extrinsic rewards. Mediating this interplay is feedback the learner receives on his or her progress in learning, both from others and as a result of self-assessments. In addition to the enjoyment of the learning task itself, intrinsic rewards also may be derived from feelings of competence, autonomy, and self-efficacy that such feedback may produce. Extrinsic rewards ranging from praise to pizza can sustain a learner's engagement when the going is difficult and progress is hard to see.

The complexity of the process of engaging and sustaining student engagement, and, in particular, the role of both intrinsic and extrinsic rewards in this process, suggest that many teachers need help in selecting and using tools that will reach more students. It is especially important to design learning environments in which students can move back and forth easily and often from intrinsic to extrinsic rewards. In this regard, it seems likely that much better use can be made of educational technology than has been made thus far.

Although finding ways to make learning tasks more intrinsically engaging is a worthwhile goal, it is extremely important that the crucial role played by extrinsic rewards in all learning is not overlooked. Much of the theory underlying educational practice in this country places heavy emphasis on engaging the interest of students. Many educators believe that undue reliance on extrinsic rewards or threats of punishment can have a negative effect on student engagement because many students will develop negative attitudes about the subject matter or will lose interest as soon as the reward or punishment is no longer effective (Shanker 1995, 49).

While there are no doubt circumstances in which extrinsic rewards can get in the way of engagement in learning, sole reliance on intrinsic rewards to engage all students all of the time is clearly unrealistic. A great deal of what students are expected to do in school involves hard work, including a variety of tasks that are regarded by most students as drudgery.

Extrinsic rewards will be necessary to sustain the engagement of many students until they achieve a level of perceived competence and autonomy that has the potential to be intrinsically engaging. In many instances, therefore, the goal must be to get students "over the hump" any way possible. Extrinsic rewards are also essential to sustain engagement when students encounter difficulties in the learning process or when tasks that initially had been interesting lose their power to engage a student's attention.

Recognition of the central role played by extrinsic rewards in all learning underscores the importance of increasing the supply of such rewards in our schools. Continuing to operate our schools as scarce reward systems, in which the best and most diligent students receive most of the rewards, contributes directly to the disengagement of many students, much of the time. Part of the problem, of course, is the inability of teachers to pay attention to and provide encouragement to all of the students for whom they are responsible, particularly at the middle and high school levels. For many students, lack of support and encouragement from parents and other potential reward-givers in our communities exacerbates this problem.

What is known about the important psychological components of intrinsic motivation and engagement in learning, including feelings of competence and autonomy on the part of the learner, highlights the need to increase opportunities for all students to perceive that they are successful at something. This notion suggests that ways must be found to broaden the range of learning experiences available to students in order to enable each learner to find something at which he or she can become proficient. The merit badge system employed by the Boy Scouts of America is an example of such an approach. In contrast to this objective, many school reformers argue that the establishment of clear expectations for student achievement in the core academic subjects, combined with regular and fair assessments of each student's progress toward meeting these expectations, is essential to increase student motivation and engagement in learning (Resnick 1995).

These two apparently contradictory perspectives present a dilemma. Assuming that all students can achieve at higher levels and providing both strong incentives for success (as well as potential punishments for failure) has the potential to energize students and teachers alike, assuming that the resources are available to give students the necessary instruction and encouragement. This approach, however, runs the risk of narrowing the range of opportunities to succeed that are available to students because of the need to concentrate available resources on those subjects that are deemed most important. In contrast, diffusion of instructional resources to accommodate a broader range of student interests could have the effect of lowering achievement in the core subjects while increasing student motivation to engage in the learning process more generally. Creating education policies and practices at the school level that take into account the need for both intrinsic and extrinsic rewards for student engagement is a formidable challenge.

5

ORGANIZING EFFORT: INCREASING THE EFFICIENCY OF LEARNING

This book began with the assertion that engagement in learning requires the expenditure of effort on the part of the learner. Implicit in this assertion is the notion that the amount of effort exerted by a learner is positively related to the amount of learning that is likely to take place, although the relationship can be complex. In the previous chapter, for example, it was noted that while the prospect of powerful extrinsic rewards or the threat of serious punishment can increase significantly the amount of effort an individual is willing to invest in a particular learning task, these rewards and punishments can also interfere with learning. At least as important a mediating factor is the effect of the learning environment, including characteristics of the learning task, on the efficiency of the learning process. Everyone has experienced situations in which the effort involved in learning is wasted or misdirected and therefore either does not result in learning or causes learning to take much longer than it might have. When this happens, motivation to stay engaged in the learning process may be eroded, if not dissipated entirely. Thus, engagement in learning is affected directly by the efficiency of the learning process.

The reasons for examining how the effort necessary to learn something is organized and expended are straightforward. Effort usefully can be regarded as an investment. The amount of effort each person has to invest in learning anything is limited; no one wants to squander his or her energies on learning strategies that are either inefficient or ineffective. This is one of the reasons why people look for good teachers or good schools for their children and for themselves when they want to learn a new skill or improve an existing skill, whether it be golf, learning to play a musical instrument, or learning a foreign language. Those who are responsible for instruction are also making an investment of valuable effort. Taken together, the amount of effort invested by both students and teachers in schools is enormous. To the extent that a significant portion of this effort is wasted, it represents both a problem and a major opportunity for increasing the overall performance of our educational system.

Effort invested in learning can be dissipated in several ways as a result of inadequately designed learning tasks or characteristics of the organizational context in which they are embedded.

1. Sustaining the engagement of learners is a major challenge in designing learning environments and specific tasks within them. If learners perceive they are not getting a return on the effort they invest in the learning process, or that the return is too low, they may stop investing.
2. Even if learners remain fully engaged in a specific learning task, some teaching methods and ways of presenting material are more effective than others. Recent advances in the cognitive sciences suggest that it is possible to do a much better (more efficient) job than is currently being done in conveying skills and knowledge to our children.
3. How learning environments—for example, school classrooms —are organized can have important effects on the efficiency and effectiveness of learning that takes place within them and, in turn, on the engagement of students.
4. The culture of the school has a significant impact on many characteristics of schools that are associated with engagement in learning, including the extent to which students identify with school values, such as the importance of academic achievement.
5. A great deal of effort is squandered because students have not learned how to manage the investment of their own efforts in the

most efficient manner. Ensuring that students learn how to learn, including the development of habits and skills that enable them to maximize the return on their efforts, is an important challenge for students, parents, and schools.

6. Finally, every classroom in every school is affected by inefficiencies in the way the education system as a whole is organized in this country.

This chapter is devoted to an examination of the ways in which characteristics of learning tasks and the context in which they are imbedded can affect the efficiency and effectiveness of learners' efforts and therefore their engagement in learning. Before turning to this task, however, it is important to note that inefficiencies in the utilization of student effort are almost certainly not equally distributed among children (or their teachers) in the nation's schools. Low-income and ethnic minority children encounter more situations in which they are at risk of investing effort without getting commensurate returns than middle- and upper-income children for whom learning tasks are often designed and who are better prepared to tackle these tasks.

THE DESIGN OF LEARNING TASKS: SUSTAINING THE ENGAGEMENT OF LEARNERS

The relationship between the design of learning tasks and the engagement of learners has several important dimensions. These include the "fit" between characteristics of learners and learning tasks, provisions incorporated (or not) into the learning environment to deal with difficulties on the part of learners, the role(s) learners are expected to play as they engage in learning, and the kinds of feedback learners receive about their performance.

The Fit between Learner and Learning Task

Chapter 2 introduced the concept of the fit between characteristics of the learners and the learning task in which they are engaged. The simplest dimension on which tasks vary, of course, is their difficulty and,

consequently, the amount of ability or advance preparation they demand on the part of the learner. Obviously, if learners do not have the
requisite ability (mental or physical) or are inadequately prepared to engage in the learning task, whatever effort they exert is likely to be
wasted. In designing learning tasks for learners of different abilities or
preparation levels, it is possible to err in two ways: by making the task
too difficult or too easy. Each type of mistake has the potential to affect
the engagement of participants. Finding the right difficulty level is compounded when one is dealing with groups of students of varying abilities
or preparation levels, as is almost always the case in school. All good
teachers (and parents) know that one solution to this problem lies in designing learning tasks that allow different students to proceed at different speeds through tasks of increasing difficulty. Computers offer the
promise of helping to solve this design problem, although realization of
their promise has been more elusive than imagined thirty years ago
when programmed instruction first came on the scene.

Even such apparently simple concepts as levels of ability and preparation for engagement in learning turn out to be more complex notions
than they appear at first glance, comprising bundles of skills that children
begin to acquire from interactions with their parents during the first five
years of life. According to the report of a committee of the National Research Council on developments in the science of learning, "parents and
others who care for children arrange their activities and facilitate learning by regulating the difficulty of the tasks and by modeling mature performance during joint participation in activities" (National Research
Council 1999). As children engage in increasingly complex learning tasks,
they also begin to learn how to connect new situations to more familiar
ones, a skill that people of all ages must have if they are to be able to
make connections among different domains of their knowledge (National
Research Council 1999, 91). In addition to differences in ability, therefore, children come to school with wide variation in their preparation for
engagement in the range of new learning tasks they will encounter.

Recent insights into the kinds of skills children acquire from interactions with their parents during the first few years of life and the relevance of these skills for learning underscore the importance and potential magnitude of disparities in preparation for school that may result
from the inability of some families, especially low income and minori-

Helping Students Choose Appropriate Reading Materials

Developed with funding from the National Institute for Child Health and Human Development (NICHD), the Lexile Framework for Reading is a set of educational tools that enables parents, teachers, and students to match readers with text (books, magazines, newspapers) that is appropriate for their reading abilities. The Lexile Framework uses software to give both readers and reading material a score called a Lexile. This allows educators (as well as students, themselves) to forecast the level of comprehension a reader will experience with a particular text.

Over 35,000 books have been given Lexile scores to date and the results of reading comprehension tests given by all of the major test publishers can be converted into Lexile scores for individual students. Developed over the last fifteen years, The Lexile Map for Reading provides a scale of reading comprehension starting with primer books like *Fox be Nimble* through postgraduate school reading such as the *New England Journal of Medicine*. Once a student knows his or her Lexile measure, the Map becomes a guide for student reading and setting goals for improvement in reading skills. The most common use of the Map is to match a student's Lexile measure to a literature title or to everyday world text, such as *The New York Times*. If, for example, a student is measured at 900 Lexiles, he or she should first look to the 900-Lexile location on the Map. Such a student would be expected to be able to read and comprehend *The Old Man and the Sea* with 75 percent comprehension.

See *The Lexile Framework* at http://www.lexile.com.

ties, to provide their children with such skills. Children whose parents do not have the resources, ability, or time to teach their children these skills start school at a considerable disadvantage compared to more affluent children. Good Head Start programs can and do help to reduce such disparities, but only about a third of the children eligible for Head Start nationally are enrolled in the program.

Some of the most vexing policy issues in the field of education revolve around the foregoing issue. Forty years ago, most kindergarten children in this country took reading readiness tests that were supposed to determine whether they were prepared to benefit from formal instruction in reading. Such tests were abandoned after research demonstrated that virtually all children have the capacity to begin learning to read in kindergarten (or earlier) and that no advantage resulted from delaying this process. The current debate over the relative efficacy of phonics versus whole language approaches to teaching reading turns on assumptions one makes about the capacity of different children to benefit from different instructional strategies. The case for phonics instruction is based on research that demonstrates clearly that some (if not all) children need the building blocks provided by phonics before they can begin to take advantage of the whole language approach to reading (U.S. Department of Health and Human Services 2000). Too much attention to phonics, in contrast, runs the risk of turning off students who have the ability and preparation necessary to derive intrinsic rewards from engagement with more complex material earlier in the educational process. As with so many of the points made thus far, the right answer lies in striking a balance that is appropriate for each student.

In the discussion of intrinsic motivation, the example of mathematics instruction in the United States and Japan was used to make the point that students approach many learning tasks with different preconceptions about whether the task will be interesting or boring, easy or difficult. Similarly, in addition to differences in ability and preparation, students bring to each learning task cognitive preconceptions that can have a profound influence on their capacity to benefit from specific learning experiences. For example, the National Research Council Committee notes that

> Students come to the classroom with preconceptions about how the world works. If their initial understanding is not engaged, they may fail to grasp the new concepts and information that are taught, or they may learn them for the purposes of a test but revert to their preconceptions outside the classroom. Research on early learning suggests that the process of making sense of the world begins at a very young age. Children begin in preschool years to develop sophisticated understandings (whether accurate or not) of the phenomena around them. Those initial understandings can have a powerful effect on the integration of new concepts and information. (National Research Council 1999, 10)

While such cognitive preconceptions are especially important for young children, learners of all ages approach each learning task with preconceptions not only about the specific task but about how the world in which they live works. "Drawing out and working with existing understandings is important for learners of all ages. Numerous research experiments demonstrate the persistence of preexisting understandings among older students even after a new model has been taught that contradicts the naïve understanding" (National Research Council 1999, 11).

Taking such preexisting conceptions and understandings into account in designing and implementing learning tasks requires awareness of the specific beliefs and ideas that students bring to the classroom, as well as knowledge of techniques that can be used to expose and challenge them in a constructive way.

Coping with Difficulties on the Part of the Learner

Not only do learners bring abilities, previous experiences, and cognitive preconceptions to any learning environment, they also bring physical characteristics and emotions that can facilitate or pose barriers to engagement in the learning process. Children may come to school ill, tired, or undernourished. They may harbor anxieties about school, their classmates, or their own capacity to learn. They may be distracted by family problems or other events outside school. Although many schools attempt to help students cope with major events and problems such as a divorce, death in the family, or serious illness, it is not easy to adapt curricula to the physical and emotional needs of individual children who present particular problems. It is impossible, moreover, for schools to compensate fully for the handicaps that result from the severe problems many children from low-income or minority families face on a day-to-day basis.

Children often are inhibited from fully engaging in learning by anxieties about their ability to succeed or fear of being ridiculed by their classmates (or, sometimes, teachers) if they make a mistake. Initiating and sustaining engagement in such situations can require substantial adaptation of learning tasks to take into account special characteristics of the student. Almost fifty years ago, the father of a young boy who was attending a summer camp where I was a swimming instructor announced to me that his only goal for his son during the ensuing two weeks was that his son learn to swim. I assured the father that this should not be a problem, but soon discovered that the boy would not go near the lake because of his fears of the water and, at least as important, failing his father. Clearly, a significant modification of the curriculum would be required if we were to get this boy engaged in this learning task and keep him engaged. Accordingly, the first several days were spent with various adults, including the camp nurse, simply sitting on the beach with the boy, each day moving closer to the water. By the fourth day, he was dipping his feet into the water, then wading up to his knees, then his waist, and, finally, floating. By the end of the two week period, he had passed his beginners' test, including diving off of the dock into deep water.

Two important conclusions can be drawn from this example. First, as all teachers know, it is often necessary to break complex, difficult, or, in this case, anxiety-producing learning tasks down into smaller, more manageable pieces and to begin with the easiest. Sometimes the pieces have to be very small indeed. Second, this kind of individualized modification of a learning task requires a very substantial investment of effort on the part of both teacher and student, and often others. Most teachers in most schools are not able to make such an investment very often, if ever. This underscores the importance of expanding significantly the number of aides, tutors, and other adults who are involved in our schools and who may be in a position to provide this kind of individualized attention.

A frequent cause of disengagement in learning is fatigue or more simply, saturation, on the part of the learner. Children, particularly younger ones, do not have unlimited attention spans, and serious engagement in learning requires the expenditure of real effort. When children run out of the energy necessary to pay attention, it is often a waste of both their and their teacher's time to try to sustain their engagement in the learning task. Yet, as quickly as children may tire of a particular task, so too are their energy levels restored with rest or a change of perspective. A great deal of experimental evidence, moreover, demonstrates that spacing out learning tasks increases the efficiency of learning significantly as compared with compressing more learning into the same period or extending the length of the period. These findings suggest it is important to closely examine the way learning activities in our schools are organized so as to maximize the amount of energy our children are able to devote to learning.

In this context, a number of useful ideas come from comparisons with other countries' educational systems. For example, although Asian children spend more time in school each day than American children, they also spend far more time than American children in recesses or at lunch. Elementary school children in this country typically have only two ten-minute breaks in the course of the school day and spend only half an hour at lunch. Asian children have several much longer breaks during the day and often take more than an hour for lunch. Longer and more frequent breaks during which children can exercise vigorously may make it possible for children to concentrate more effectively when they are in class, and therefore to make much more efficient use of instructional time.

Learners' Roles and Their Motivation to Engage in Learning

Conventional wisdom in the field of education, dating at least from the time of Socrates, holds that active participation of the learner in the learning process increases student engagement and therefore learning. Active participation on the part of students in the classroom may involve responding to questions posed by the instructor or participation in discussions in which the student has an opportunity to express his or her own opinions (Wagner 2002). There is ample evidence that involving learners actively in the process of learning helps to sustain their engagement. In 1996, Herbert Simon noted that

Discovery learning gets students to work on interesting situations that motivate them to discover for themselves certain underlying concepts and connections. Research on curiosity tells us that people will stop attending to a stimulus if it is so simple it becomes boring, or so complex it appears chaotic and meaningless. A well-designed discovery learning experience can introduce children to what scientists do and how they go about doing it, for example, and can be more motivating than a traditional lecture approach. But discovery learning is not an automatic motivator. Research indicates that in order to be effective, discovery learning

experiences must strike the right balance between simplicity and complexity, build on the previous knowledge and experience of the learner,
and offer opportunities for discovery at a pace that sustains student interest. (Simon 1996)

Current views of maximally effective learning environments also suggest that such environments must encourage and enable learners to do
far more than accumulate facts. In *Making the Grade*, Tony Wagner
(2002, 91) describes the five "habits of mind" developed by Deborah
Meier, principal of the Central Park East Secondary School in Manhat-
tan, and her teachers, as follows:

- *Weighing evidence*: How do we know what we know? What is the evidence and is it credible?
- *Awareness of varying viewpoints*: What viewpoint are we hearing, seeing, reading? Who is the author and what are his or her intentions?
- *Seeing connections and relationships*: How are things connected to each
  other? Where have we heard or seen this before?
- *Speculating on possibilities*: What if . . . ? Can we imagine alternatives?
- *Assessing value both socially and personally*: What difference does it
  make? Who cares?

A number of observers have also noted that enabling learners to shift
roles during learning can help to sustain their engagement in the learning task. One dimension of the way in which lessons are organized
within the classroom relates to the distinction between class work and
seat work. Activities in the classroom, for example, can be grouped into
those in which the teacher is working with all of the students, lecturing
or leading a discussion, and those in which students work individually or
in small groups on assigned tasks. The opportunity to shift from one type
of organizational arrangement to another during a single lesson helps to
sustain the engagement of learners in the learning task (Stigler and
Hiebert 1999).

In their theoretical work on the design of effective learning environments, Moore and Anderson (1969) suggest that all learning environments enable learners to take one or more of four perspectives on the
task or activity in which they are engaged. These perspectives are:

1. The "agent perspective," which enables the learner to experience his or her effect on or control over the environment (for example, conducting an experiment or solving a problem),
2. The "patient perspective," in which the learner is subject to events over which he or she has no control (for example, listening to a lecture or watching a film),
3. The "reciprocal perspective," which requires learners to take account of the behavior of others (for example, participating as a member of a team), and
4. The "referees' perspective," which affords the learner an opportunity to make normative judgments about the behavior of others, events, or objects (for example, having responsibility for organizing an activity or enforcing rules).

Moore and Anderson further hypothesize that "one environment is more conducive to learning than another if it both permits and facilitates the taking of more perspectives toward whatever it is to be learned" (Moore and Anderson 1969, 585). Moreover, they suggest that limitations on the attention span of children should more properly be viewed as limitations of their "perspective span." Designing learning tasks that allow children (or adults, for that matter) to shift perspectives should, according to Moore and Anderson, increase significantly the length of time that they will stay engaged in any particular task.

Feedback Learners Receive on Their Performance

A crucially important dimension of all learning environments and the tasks embedded within them is how they are structured to provide learners with feedback on their performance. Many different things fall into the category of feedback on student performance. At one end of the spectrum are informal comments by teachers and others, including classmates, that occur frequently. At the other extreme are formal reports, including grades and written appraisals of performance, standardized test scores, and comparative rankings such as the student's standing in class. In between are evaluations of products generated in the normal course of the learning process, ranging from papers to portfolios, grades on informal tests given by teachers, and assorted other evidence of a student's proficiency and performance.

Most appraisals relate to the work of individual students but as students increasingly work in teams, they may receive grades that reflect the work of several students.

Regular and frequent feedback to students on their progress is an integral part of every learning environment. The feedback learners receive on their performance is an essential component of both intrinsic and extrinsic rewards that help to sustain learner engagement in any learning task. Such feedback also is necessary to enable students to improve their performance. Frequent assessments of a learner's progress, moreover, help teachers to modify instructional practices to better meet the needs of their pupils. Beyond this consensus, however, there is considerable debate about how best to accomplish these objectives.

Among the issues that must be addressed are what aspects of student performance are most important to keep track of and to provide feedback to students on. Another is the potential for conflict between performance appraisal systems designed to inform students about their progress and those whose primary function is to assess the performance of schools or school systems. Increased emphasis on the accountability of schools for the performance of their students is certain to have a significant influence on what is taught and on the ways in which student performance is measured. Scores on standardized tests that are designed primarily to measure a school's progress in making sure that its students meet statewide standards may have little meaning to many individual students and therefore be less likely than other kinds of feedback to sustain their motivation to work hard in school. Such scores also may not be very helpful to teachers in diagnosing strengths and weakness of individual students, or in enabling them to modify teaching methods to meet those needs (Wagner 2002). So-called authentic measures of achievement based on students' performance on real-world tasks, on the other hand, may be motivating to students and teachers, but less useful to either parents or state legislators in deciding how well a school is doing at imparting basic skills to their children.

Perhaps most important, attaching real consequences ("high stakes"), such as graduation from high school or increased funding for schools, to the results of a few standardized tests has the potential to further limit the range of extrinsic rewards available to students by focusing everyone's attention on a relatively narrow range of competencies. It seems clear that more attention needs to be given to mechanisms, both formal and informal, used to inform students, as well as their parents, about how well they are doing in school. At the forefront of any such consideration should be a focus on their implications for student engagement and motivation.

THE ORGANIZATION OF LEARNING IN AMERICAN SCHOOLS

How learning is organized in American classrooms has a major influence on the efficiency of both teachers' and students' effort. Several aspects of learning environments can affect that efficiency: the relative responsibilities of teachers and students for learning, the amount and type of learning expected of students, the degree to which different parts of the learning environment fit together, the extent to which different learning environments complement and reinforce one another, and the amount of time available for learning.

The Responsibilities of Students and Teachers

Active involvement of students in the learning process is positively associated with student motivation, engagement, and, ultimately, learning, although it is not completely clear what "active involvement" means. Earlier, the importance of opportunities for learners to shift roles and perspectives for sustaining their motivation and engagement in the learning process was discussed. Here I turn to the question of the respective responsibilities of teachers and students for what happens within any learning environment. At one extreme, one can imagine situations in which the primary responsibility for instruction rests with the teacher; near the other end of the spectrum, students are required to assume much greater responsibility for their own learning. In the first instance, for example, the teacher provides information or demonstrates a method for solving a problem; students are responsible for paying attention to what the teacher says and then practicing what they have learned. In the latter case, students might be asked to find relevant information on their own or to develop alternative ways of solving a problem for which they have not been given a solution.

Most people can probably remember instances in which they have been engaged in each of the foregoing types of learning environments. Many learning environments, moreover, blend aspects of each. Comparative studies of schools in the United States and other countries, especially China, Japan, and Germany, however, suggest that situations in which teachers take primary responsibility are more common in American schools than situations in which students assume primary responsibility for their own learning (Stevenson and Stigler 1992; Stigler and Hiebert 1999). One reason for this difference may be that it is common practice in our schools to separate instruction in basic skills from more complex problem-solving activities. In the past, many educators argued that students must acquire basic skills before they can progress to more advanced types of learning. Recent research reveals, however, that even very young children pose questions, test hypotheses, and engage in other complex reasoning skills once thought beyond their abilities (National Research Council 1999, 1999a). These newer findings suggest that motivation and engagement in learning can be negatively affected by requiring children to master basic skills and subskills before allowing them to engage in richer, more complex tasks.

Finding the right balance between expecting children to take too much responsibility for their own learning and not giving them enough depends, in part, on the experience and capabilities of the learner. At the same time, lessons from abroad suggest that we may have underestimated the capacity of children to play a more active role and to become engaged in more complex problem-solving activities at earlier stages in the learning process.

Expectations for Student Learning

The idea that most children should have opportunities to play a more active role in learning is reinforced by new understandings about the learning process itself and about what is necessary to develop real competence in any domain of knowledge (National Research Council 1999, 1999b). Studies of the performance of experts as compared with novices, along with research on how expertise in one domain transfers to another domain, lead to the conclusion that knowledge of a set of disconnected facts is not sufficient to enable learners to make use of their knowledge in any meaningful way. A recent report of a committee of the National Research Council summarizes the results of this research as follows:

> To develop competence in an area of inquiry, students must have opportunities to learn with understanding. Deep understanding of subject matter transforms factual information into usable knowledge. A pronounced difference between experts and novices is that experts' command of concepts shapes their understanding of new information: it allows them to see patterns, relationships, or discrepancies that are not apparent to novices. They do not necessarily have better memories than other people. But their conceptual understanding allows them to extract a level of meaning from information that is not apparent to novices, and this helps them select and remember relevant information. (National Research Council 1999b, 12)

The NRC committee further noted that "A key finding in the learning and transfer literature is that organizing information into a conceptual framework allows for greater 'transfer'; that is, it allows the student to apply what was learned in new situations and to learn related information more quickly" (National Research Council 1999b, 12–13).

The committee's conclusion was that "To develop competence in an area of inquiry, students must: (a) have a deep foundation of factual knowledge, (b) understand facts and ideas in the context of a conceptual framework, and (c) organize knowledge in ways that facilitate retrieval and application" (National Research Council 1999b, 12).

In the previous chapter, it was pointed out that a learner's sense of competence and autonomy underlie his engagement in learning activities in which rewards are primarily intrinsic to the learning task. The foregoing observations about what constitutes "competence" in an area of inquiry (or skill) suggest the kinds of learning that are necessary if learners are to make the transition from extrinsic to intrinsic motivation, thereby increasing significantly the efficiency of the learning process.

How Schools Are Organized

Throughout the course of a typical school day, students participate in a series of learning activities and environments. Even though elementary students may remain in the same classroom for most of the day, the day is divided into different segments, each one focused on a different subject. Within each subject, in turn, students encounter a variety of different learning activities and tasks. At the middle and high school levels, students not only are changing subjects throughout the day, they are usually changing classrooms and teachers, as well. The ability of students to stay focused and therefore engaged in any particular learning activity depends to a significant extent on the coherence of that activity, as well as its relationship to other learning tasks and activities that are going on around it.

One of the things that Stevenson and Stigler (1992) observed in their comparative study of Asian versus American classrooms was the degree of coherence in the way in which lessons were organized and presented in the different countries. In thinking about the coherence of lessons, they use the analogy of a story, as follows:

> A good story is highly organized; it has a beginning, a middle, and an end, and it follows a protagonist who meets challenges and resolves problems that arise along the way. Above all, a good story engages the reader's interest in a series of interconnected events, each of which is best understood in the context of the events that precede and follow it.
>
> In Asia, instruction is guided by this concept of a lesson. The curricula include coherent lessons, each carefully designed to fill a forty- to fifty-minute class period with sustained attention to the development of some concept or skill. Like a good story, the lesson has an introduction, a conclusion, and a consistent theme. (Stevenson and Stigler 1992, 177)

A Fifth-Grade Mathematics Lesson in Japan

The teacher walks in carrying a large paper bag full of clinking glass. Her entry into the classroom with a large paper bag is highly unusual, and by the time she has placed it on her desk, the students are regarding her with rapt attention. What's in the bag? She begins to pull out items, placing them one by one on her desk. She removes a pitcher and a vase. A beer bottle evokes laughter and surprise. She soon has six containers lined up on her desk. The children continue to watch intently, glancing back and forth at each other as they seek to understand the purpose of this display.

The teacher, looking thoughtfully at the containers, poses a question: "I wonder which one would hold the most water?" Hands go up, and the teacher calls on different students to give their guesses: "the pitcher," "the beer bottle," "the teapot." The teacher stands aside and ponders: "Some of you said one thing, others said something different. You don't agree with one another. There must be some way we can find out who is correct. How can we know who is correct?" Interest is high, and the discussion continues.

The students soon agree that to find out how much each container holds, they will need to fill the containers with something. How about water? The teacher finds some buckets and sends several children out to fill them with water. When they return, the teacher says: "Now what do we do?" Again there is a discussion, and after several minutes the children decide that they will need to use a smaller container to measure how much water fits into each of the larger containers. They decide on a drinking cup, and one of the students warns that they all have to fill each cup to the same level—otherwise the measure won't be the same for all the groups.

At this point, the teacher divides the class into their groups and gives each group one of the containers and a drinking cup. Each group fills its container, counts how many cups of water it holds, and writes the result in a notebook. When all the groups have completed the task, the teacher calls on the leader of each group to report on its findings, and notes the results on the blackboard. She has written the names of the containers in a column on the left and a scale from 1 to 6 along the bottom. As each group makes its report, the teacher draws a bar representing the amount the container holds: pitcher, 4.5 cups; vase, 3 cups, beer bottle, 1.5 cups; and so on.

Finally the teacher returns to the question she posed at the beginning of the lesson: Which container holds the most water? She reviews how they were able to solve the problem, and points out that the answer is now contained in the bar graph on the board. She then arranges the containers on the table according to how much they hold, and writes a rank order on each container, from 1 to 6. She ends the class with a brief review of what they have done. No definitions of ordinate and abscissa, no discussion of how to make a graph preceded the example—these all became obvious in the course of the lesson, and only at the end did the teacher mention the terms that describe the horizontal and vertical axes of the graph they had made.

Excerpt from Harold W. Stevenson and James W. Stigler, *The Learning Gap* (New York: Simon and Schuster, Touchstone Books, 1992), 177–78.

Asian teachers are also far more likely than American teachers to organize their lessons around a problem that requires students to recognize what is known and what is unknown, and to direct the students' attention to the critical parts of the problem. Even mechanics such as
mathematical computation are usually presented in the context of solving a problem.

In contrast, the lessons that Stevenson and Stigler observed in American classrooms were much more likely to lack coherence, even when
the lessons had obviously been carefully planned. Teachers, for example, more often failed to relate different parts of the lesson to one another, or to summarize the purpose of the lesson at the end. In American classrooms, lessons were frequently interrupted both by digressions
taken by the teacher during the lesson and by intrusions from outside
the classroom (including frequent announcements over the school's in-
tercom). American teachers also had a much greater tendency to shift
topics during the course of a single lesson.

Almost a decade after Stevenson and Stigler's descriptions of the
coherence of Asian lessons, Stigler and Hiebert (1999) returned to
the same topic in their comparative examination of mathematics
teaching in several countries, including Japan, Germany, and the
United States. As in the earlier report, they observed that classroom
lessons "hold a privileged place" in Japanese schools; they are
"treated much as we treat lectures in university courses or religious
services in church" and a great deal of effort goes into their planning.
In part because of this emphasis on coherence, they are almost never
interrupted by anything in Japanese schools. Mathematics lessons in
the United States, however, are more modular in character, with
fewer interconnections among their components (Stigler and Hiebert
1999, 96).

What conclusions should be drawn from these observations in the
context of a focus on motivation and engagement? It seems clear that
American classrooms and teaching practices pose more challenges to
student engagement and sustained attention to learning tasks, as well
as efficiency in the utilization of effort, than do teaching practices in
some other countries. I shall return to this issue in the discussion of
the problem of the amount of time available for learning in American
schools.

Taking Advantage of Opportunities for Synergies among Learning Tasks

The diversity of learning tasks and experiences that students encounter in school means that students rarely have an opportunity to sustain their engagement in any particular learning task for very long. Students are constantly shifting their attention among the subjects they are studying in school, not to mention the wide variety of activities in which they are engaged outside of school (see chapter 7). While this may help to prevent boredom, it also makes it difficult for students to pursue more deeply those subjects that most interest them or to understand and appreciate connections that exist among different domains of knowledge.

In the view of many observers, the lack of intellectual coherence among the courses most students take, particularly at the high school level, is an especially important problem. According to Ted Sizer,

> One of the curses of the current system is that it is incoherent. Even the physics course has initially nothing to do with the math course, much less art and English. The current debate over standards assumes the fixed position of the well-established, one-hundred-year-old subject matters. . . . Unless there is some interweaving of subject matter, all of this effort [toward developing academic standards] is going to go for naught. (Holton and Goroff 1995)

Designing learning tasks that combine work in different subjects could increase the intellectual coherence among courses, as well as help to integrate standards for student achievement across disciplines. Both writing and mathematics, for example, can be taught using examples from other subjects in the curriculum, such as science, social studies, history, and geography. Combining subjects in this way has obvious efficiency advantages. Furthermore, it may make it possible to sustain the engagement of students in complex learning tasks over longer periods of time.

Time Available for Learning

It almost goes without saying that learning is a function of the amount of time learners are able to invest in the learning process. This is always the case when one is attempting to learn complex skills, acquire a large body of knowledge, or develop an understanding of the relationships among a number of variables. Everyone can think of instances in which he or she learned something very quickly, but such cases almost always involve acquisition of a discrete piece of information or very simple skill. Sometimes one perceives that learning has taken place almost instantaneously when, in fact, what has occurred is a sudden insight imbedded in and resulting from a much longer process of learning. Whatever caveats are placed on the statement of the relationship between time and learning, however, there is no doubt that one of the most important variables affecting the outcome of the learning process is the amount of quality time the learner invests in it. The amount of time the learner invests, in turn, is determined by the learner's motivation to engage in the learning process and the amount of time that is available. This basic principle leads to a consideration of a number of important aspects of the relationship between the time available for learning and the engagement of learners in our schools.

The first of these dimensions of the relationship between time and learner engagement is the quality of the time spent on the task. In 1985, another committee of the National Research Council, this one focused on mathematics, science, and technology education, observed that

> Although other factors enter importantly into an effective education, a powerful factor influencing school learning is the amount of class time devoted to active teaching and learning of relevant skills—called "quality learning time" in this report. The importance of quality learning time is reflected in a core set of findings about the effectiveness of alternative learning conditions. More concentration on a subject leads to higher student performance. Greater amounts of time spent by students on active learning leads to higher achievement. Given the curriculum materials in current use and the usual procedure of teacher-led group instruction, supervised learning activities involving substantive interaction between teacher and students is more effective than unsupervised instruction. (National Research Council 1985, 3)

The committee's conclusion is consistent with several of the points made earlier in this chapter. It underscores the thesis underlying this book: namely, that learning anything complex is serious business, re-

quiring concentration and effort on the part of both students and teachers. The concept of quality time spent on the task captures the idea that
simply attending a mathematics class is not necessarily more likely to result in learning mathematics than putting one's math book underneath
one's pillow at night.

One of the important implications of this observation is that most data
on the amount of instruction children receive in different subjects in our
schools seriously overstate the amount of quality time they actually spend
on learning. Such data are based on total hours formally allocated to different subjects in the course of a year; they do not reflect what actually
happens in classrooms, much less whether any particular child or group
of children is actively engaged in learning at any given time. Observational data suggest that a relatively small portion of the time devoted to
instruction in American classrooms can be characterized as quality time
on the task, even for a subset of the children in the classroom. Stephen
Graubard described his experience in a school classroom as follows:

> I was struck by the extraordinary amount of time school teachers spent
> keeping order in the classroom. It was not a matter of preventing students
> from throwing spitballs—such behavior might have happened at any
> time—but of keeping some modicum of order in the classroom. Making
> certain that everyone had the paper and the books required took time.
> "Teach, I don't have a pencil," cried one boy. Out came the pencil, deliv-
> ered with only a very slight hint of impatience. Other equally urgent re-
> quests were also attended to. Forty-five minutes, interrupted by more
> than occasional messages from the public address system, passed very
> quickly. The teaching was minimal. (Graubard 1995, 32)

The way time available for learning is structured also has an important potential impact on the motivation and engagement of learners. In
describing learning in America as "a prisoner of time," the report of the
National Education Commission on Time and Learning observed that
"for the past 150 years American schools have held time constant and
let learning vary" (National Education Commission on Time and
Learning 1994, 7). The commission's report points out that "if experience, research, and common sense teach nothing else, they confirm the
truism that people learn at different rates and in different ways with
different subjects." Despite this fact, schools for the most part operate

on a fixed schedule, with approximately 5.6 hours of classes per day, 180 days per year. Most classes are fifty-one minutes long and rarely is there any flexibility in the schedule that would allow extra time for students who needed more time. According to the National Education Commission report,

> students are processed on an assembly line, scheduled to the minute. Our usage of time virtually assures the failure of many students.
>
> • Under today's practices, high-ability students are forced to spend more time than they need on a curriculum developed for students of moderate ability. They end up bored, unmotivated, and frustrated.
> • Struggling students are forced to move with the class and receive less time than they need to master the material.
> • Average students are caught in a time trap, as well. Good teachers try to keep their best students motivated and help slow students. Average students, therefore, are likely to be overlooked. (15)

Finally, the total amount of time spent on instruction in American schools is limited. The National Education Commission report cites data that, on average, only 41 percent of the time secondary school students spend in class is devoted to academic core subjects. Thus, of the 5.6 hours of classes per day, only about 2.5 hours is spent on core academic subjects—a total of 450 hours per year. Moreover, according to the National Education Commission, these hours are being eroded every year as more time is allocated to nonacademic activities in many schools. Taking into account the fact that quality learning time on task for most students represents only a fraction of these hours, the amount of engaged learning time could be as low as 200 hours a year or less. Other countries protect academic time, with students commonly receiving twice as much instruction in core academic subjects (see table, National Education Commission on Time and Learning 1994, 24).

Time Available for Teachers

If the limitations on time available to students are severe, the situation for teachers is much worse. With responsibility for teaching 150 or more students in several different courses each day at the secondary school level, most teachers are stretched to the limit of their capabilities and beyond. Few teachers can find the time to do the kind of careful preparation of lessons that characterizes schools in some other countries or to think about ways to improve what they are currently doing. On top of these burdens, many school systems are making demands on teachers to participate in a wide range of activities associated with school reform and improvement efforts. According to a RAND study, new teaching strategies can require as much as fifty hours of instruction, practice, and coaching before teachers are comfortable with them (National Education Commission on Time and Learning 1994). The conclusion is inescapable: the nation's 2.75 million teachers do not have the time they need to keep pace with changing standards while continuing to teach their students.

Time Spent on Learning Outside of School

Quality time spent on learning tasks in school is not the only time children spend engaged in learning academic subjects. Most students spend some time on a regular basis outside of school engaged in school-related learning tasks. Outside-of-school learning time is spent on homework, studying for tests, and other school-related activities, including reading, watching education-related television, using computers, and participating in academic-related extracurricular activities such as the science or math club. The amount of time students spend doing homework and studying for tests is directly related to the demands placed on them by their teachers and the stringency with which these demands are enforced.

Expectations for student work outside school increase steadily from elementary to middle to high school in the United States. At the same time, there is great variation in the amount of work outside school expected at all levels, based on the courses students take, teacher styles, and standards set by schools and school systems. Overall, recent data suggest that high school students spend on average less than five hours a week engaged in activities directly related to coursework in school—for example, homework and studying for tests. Many observers have noted that this is less than one-third the amount of time children report watching television (Thomas 1993).

Not only is there great variation in the amount of time spent by different students, there are also significant differences among students in the way in which this time is used. These differences help to account for the fact that numerous studies have failed to demonstrate a strong relationship between the amount of time students report spending on homework and achievement in school (Thomas 1993).

THE IMPORTANCE OF SCHOOL CLIMATE

Over the last twenty years, a considerable body of evidence has accumulated suggesting that the way in which schools are organized and operated and, in particular, the resulting school climate has an important effect on student engagement in learning. Much of this research has revealed significant differences in student motivation and engagement in learning between large bureaucratically organized schools and smaller, more communally organized schools (Wagner 2002; National Research Council 2003). These are not surprising findings, given everything that is known about the important part played by culture and cultural values in influencing human behavior. Like every organization, each school develops its own culture and sets of rules that help to govern the behavior of everyone involved in it, students and teachers alike.

It is clear that schools can and do differ greatly in the degree to which their culture ("climate") values academic achievement and encourages engagement in learning on the part of all students in the school. In some schools, there is little sense of shared commitment to the importance of academic achievement. Individual teachers are left largely on their own to motivate their students, to enforce their own rules of conduct, and to build separate cultures of academic achievement within each classroom. Inevitably, some succeed and some fail to engage their students. Other schools deliberately seek to create a common sense of community and an overall culture that is supportive of the learning enterprise.

Communally organized schools have several important characteristics including a collective sense of responsibility on the part of teachers for the education of their students; a feeling on the part of students that teachers care about them; a common sense of purpose on the part of both students and teachers; a sense of belonging on the part of all students; a high degree of relational trust among students, teachers, administrators, and parents; meaningful relationships between students and adults within the school; and a perception of fairness on the part of students concerning the way in which the school treats them. Most important, students identify with school values, including the importance of academic achievement. Studies have shown that teachers in schools with these characteristics have higher morale, greater satisfaction with their jobs, and lower absenteeism. Similarly, students report being more engaged in learning, have lower dropout rates, and are less likely to cut classes (National Research Council 2003).

These differences between communally organized schools and more traditional bureaucratically organized schools are most striking at the high school level, in large part because the size and diversity of many American high schools today makes the development of a common sense of community and single culture much more difficult. The consolidation of high schools in this country over the last fifty years has resulted in the fact that many high schools currently enroll more than 1,500 students. Schools as large as 5,000 students are not uncommon, particularly in large urban and suburban school districts. Building a real sense of community in such a large organization, particularly one with a transient student population, is a formidable challenge and one that not many large schools are able to meet. This fact has given impetus to the recent movement within education supported in part by the Gates Foundation to create smaller schools at the high school level (Wagner 2002).

An important additional dimension of school climate that is associated with increased engagement of students in learning is what has come to be called "academic press." This concept connects high expectations for student achievement on the part of everyone in the school community to the shared sense of commitment to academic goals. Without the incorporation of strong expectations for academic achievement on the part of all members of the community, the other elements of the communal model are unlikely to produce significant positive effects on academic achievement.

It seems clear that essential ingredients for increasing student engagement in learning include both high expectations for academic performance and an environment in which students feel connected to one another, as well as their teachers. Relying on high standards alone to improve the performance of students and schools seems likely to fail. The challenge for schools, therefore, is to couple increased expectations for student performance with the creation of learning environments that nurture close and caring relationships among students, teachers and other school personnel, as well as parents. Meeting this challenge will require schools and school systems to rethink in fundamental ways not only what they expect of their students, but also how schools are organized and managed. I shall return to this issue in chapter 8.

LEARNING HOW TO USE EFFORT

Not all time spent engaged in learning tasks generates the same amount of learning. In addition to variations in sheer levels of energy expended—for example, how hard one concentrates on a task—there is a great deal of evidence that the specific activities and strategies people use when they are engaged in learning can significantly increase or decrease the efficiency of the learning process. These activities and strategies include techniques for increasing the retention of whatever it is one is trying to learn (study aids), metacognition and task-monitoring strategies, and effort-management strategies (Thomas 1993). Individuals can be taught many of these techniques and strategies for increasing the efficiency and effectiveness of the ways they expend effort in learning. Little systematic attention, however, is given to helping children acquire and utilize these skills in this country.

Study Aids

A major principle that emerges from studies of human cognition, learning, and memory is that retention of complex information is much easier if the learner is able to organize the information in some meaningful way. Many of the techniques learners use to organize and record important information derive from this principle. Outlining, note taking, and identifying and categorizing key information all help learners to encode, select, and integrate information in ways that facilitate learning and longer-term retention of information (Thomas 1993).

College students typically make extensive use of such techniques to increase their comprehension and retention of course material. Elementary and secondary school students, however, are much less likely to employ such techniques systematically, nor do most schools make any effort to teach students these skills. The result, Thomas (1993) notes, is that "although it's clear from laboratory studies that constructing study aids such as summaries and outlines significantly improves adolescents' comprehension, memory, and problem-solving performance, the spontaneous use of such techniques is the exception rather than the rule in secondary level courses" (Thomas 1993, 116).

Metacognition and Task-Monitoring Strategies

"A 'metacognitive' approach to instruction can help students learn to take control of their own learning by defining learning goals and monitoring their progress in achieving them" (National Research Council 1999b, 13). Metacognitive learning strategies often take the form of a conversation internal to the learner, in which the learner monitors his or her own progress, identifies gaps in knowledge or needed improvements in skills, observes which solutions to problems encountered are most successful, and sets goals for future learning activities. Many students develop such internal dialogs on their own, but "research suggests that children can be taught these strategies, including the ability to predict outcomes, explain to oneself in order to improve understanding, note failures to comprehend, activate background knowledge, plan ahead, and apportion time and memory" (National Research Council 1999b, 14). An example of the employment of such a strategy would be a student assessing his or her strengths and weaknesses in preparing for a forthcoming examination and focusing effort on areas of greatest weakness. It is worth noting that metacognitive activities would appear to be centrally important in the process by which learners set goals for themselves, and therefore also linked to intrinsic motivation and engagement.

Despite increased awareness of the important role played by metacognitive and task-monitoring strategies in learning, there is evidence that relatively few students make systematic use of such strategies on a regular basis. For example, studies of the strategies used by students while reading or studying suggest that both high school and college students "exhibit fairly low levels of comprehension monitoring"

—that is, paying attention to differences in the level of difficulty of what they are reading or to anomalies in the text. Many students also fail to take into account the demands of learning tasks or to adapt study strategies to their perception of these demands (Thomas 1993, 144).

Effort-Management Strategies

Similarly, as most parents are aware, few high school students pay much attention to studying efficiently or to managing the time that they spend doing schoolwork, as compared with other activities. In one study, only 25 percent of high school seniors reported that they usually or always had a schedule or plan in which they set aside time on a regular basis for homework. In the same study, half of students in the ninth and twelfth grades reported that they typically studied while listening to music or watching TV. In part, this is a function of the demands made on students by the educational system. There is evidence, for example, that higher expectations and demands for student performance prompt greater student effort and higher achievement, so long as the goals are perceived as achievable. Students also must have a clear understanding of what is expected of them.

THE GOALS OF PUBLIC EDUCATION AND THE ORGANIZATION OF SCHOOLS

Finally, it is necessary to consider a set of cultural beliefs about the goals of education and how it should be conducted in this country that have very important implications both for what is taught and the methods used to teach in American schools. These issues have significant potential to affect the efficiency and effectiveness of learning processes and therefore on the return American students and their parents receive on their investments in learning.

Many of the most important characteristics of American schools and the educational system in general are driven by deeply rooted beliefs in the importance and uniqueness of each individual. The most commonly articulated goal of American education is to maximize the potential of each child. This goal, coupled with recognition of and beliefs in the importance of individual differences, profoundly affects virtually every aspect of the U.S. educational system and the schools within it. Not only do Americans believe that each child is unique and has unique potential, they want their children's teachers and schools to do everything possible to ensure that each child realizes his or her full potential. These beliefs mean that, ideally, every child would receive instruction, support, and encouragement designed specifically for his or her abilities and needs. They also lead to a deep suspicion of any one-size-fits-all approach to anything having to do with schools, from curriculum design to teaching methods to student assessment.

These beliefs and the policies that result from them create significant inequities in the opportunities available to students in American schools. Many students benefit in important ways from the special attention, encouragement, and individualized instruction they receive from their teachers and others within their schools. Many others do not. Because there are not enough teachers to provide individualized attention to more than a few students in their classes, many students do not receive these benefits. Those students who, as a result of encouragement from a teacher or their own initiative, are fortunate enough to become deeply engaged in one or more areas of interest and to develop a sense of competence and self-efficacy are set on a path that is very likely to lead them to success in school and beyond. In contrast, students who begin with doubts about their own competence and ability to succeed in school and who therefore may be most in need of encouragement from teachers are least likely to receive it.

Another natural consequence of a focus on individual differences in abilities and learning styles is to encourage teachers to develop their own methods for teaching different students. The more teachers develop their own methods and adaptations of the curriculum in order to appeal to particular students' interests and needs, the more idiosyncratic the learning environment becomes. In such an environment, determining those students who will encounter good teachers using effective teaching methods and those students who will not is left largely to chance or to the effective use of the parents' grapevine to identify the best teachers in their children's school. In any case, many students are shortchanged.

The American philosophy of emphasizing the importance of individual differences is not the only possible basis on which an educational system can be structured. In contrast to the American model, educators in China and Japan take the view that all children can benefit from a common educational experience and that it is not necessary to consider individual differences in setting curricular goals and in developing educational programs (Stevenson and Stigler 1992).

The Lack of a Common Curriculum

The cultural emphasis on the importance of individual differences is consistent with another of the most fiercely held tenets of American education: namely, the inviolability of the concept of local control of schools. Every state, and within states many local school districts, is responsible for developing its own curriculum. In each school district, boards of education and superintendents set policies and procedures that govern much of what happens in and out of classrooms across the system on a daily basis. Local districts and the schools within them are responsible for hiring, assigning, promoting, compensating, and firing teachers and other staff. Aside from state-mandated tests, they determine what tests will be used to assess pupil performance on a regular basis. They determine schedules, organize field trips, get students to and from schools, and are responsible for a host of other decisions that affect the learning environment and the students who participate in it.

The resistance in this country to anything that smacks of centralized control of local schools is deeply embedded in the culture. The roots of these beliefs can be traced to the principles, values, and ideals that brought people to these shores in the beginning and have attracted generations of immigrants ever since. Central to these beliefs are the principles that protect the freedoms Americans have to express themselves as they choose and to maintain their cultural heritage, among others. The lack, however, of some mechanism for promoting consistency, if not uniformity, in at least some aspects of what children are taught and expected to learn, and in the way they are taught, has important consequences for both individuals and the society as a whole. The negative effects of this lack of uniformity in the curricula of American schools are exacerbated by the unequal distribution of resources available to run our schools (Kozol 1991).

In addition to inequities in opportunities to become engaged in learning, the decentralization of control over what goes on in schools is enormously inefficient, and therefore extraordinarily wasteful of the efforts of everyone involved, including students. As noted above, every state must develop its own educational goals and then adopt standards for the achievement of these goals. Each school system must design a curriculum to reach these goals and then figure out how to implement it. Every state and many school systems must decide what textbooks to buy and how to use them. Every teacher must design his or her lessons and homework assignments and assessments of student performance, usually with minimal assistance from anyone else. The list of things that vary from teacher to teacher, from classroom to classroom, from school to school, and from state to state is very long. The amount of time spent every year on creating and re-creating, classroom by classroom and school system by school system, so many of the things that comprise the process of education is staggering. Such an investment might even be worthwhile if it resulted in continuous improvement of the way schools are organized and the instruction children receive. The outcome, however, is almost certainly just the opposite. This process is guaranteed only to prevent schools and teachers from benefiting from previous experience, from adopting methods that have been proven to be successful, and from taking advantage of the results of research and development (Stevenson and Stigler 1992; Shanker 1995).

When one stops to think about it, it is remarkable that such a system could exist (and has existed for a century or more) in the country that is responsible for inventing standardized procedures for almost every aspect of the society, from manufacturing to service delivery. In every other area of American life, great stock is placed in the efficiencies that result from standardization, mass production, and economies of scale. Great value always has been placed on the work of skilled artisans who produce handmade sweaters, furniture, or jewelry. And the unique contributions of individual inventors, scientists, artists, and writers will always be revered. At the same time, Americans have come to appreciate the fact that almost everything from fast food to refrigerators, automobiles, and airplanes can be produced much less expensively and with much greater reliability if they are all made the same way. At least as important, they have learned that it is possible to keep making them better through systematic investments in research and development.

Obviously, children are different from automobiles and no one is suggesting that schools be transformed into assembly lines, complete with robot instructors. It is important to recognize, however, that the country is paying a high price and receiving, at best, inconsistent quality, for its insistence on local control over much of what happens in its schools and for the simultaneous unrealistic demand that all children receive high-quality, individualized instruction. Paradoxically, the insistence on de-centralization and individualization of the educational process makes it far more difficult for teachers to find the time to do what they are supposed to be doing: namely, to teach their students. As Albert Shanker has pointed out,

> When all teachers at a grade level or in a subject are teaching a common curriculum, there is a basis for professional discussion and collegiality, which we now lack. Which approaches and which materials work best and with whom? Moreover, teachers can be trained to teach a particular subject, texts can be targeted, and many lessons can be standardized and techniques routinized. Is this "unprofessional"? Quite the contrary. Every profession relies on proven, standard operating procedures. Imagine a doctor, a pharmacist, or an engineer—or even a barber— constantly having to be inventive. Creativity comes into play in difficult, non-routine situations and in developing a better set of routines. The notion that standardization and routinization are evils and that teachers should be creative and innovative every minute of the day is disastrous. It is also a major barrier to transforming teaching into a genuine profession. (Shanker 1995, 52–53)

The inefficiencies inherent in American schools also make it more difficult for teachers to give all of their students the attention they need. Increasing children's engagement in learning tasks requires the availability of more, not fewer, extrinsic rewards, including encouragement by teachers. To achieve this goal, ways must be found to make the instructional process itself both more efficient and more effective, thus enabling teachers to spend more time paying attention to their students and thereby sustaining their engagement in the learning process.

Lesson Planning

One of the most important inefficiencies in American education occurs at the classroom level. At the heart of the educational system is what teachers do each day to teach their students whatever it is that they are supposed to learn. Perhaps the most remarkable fact about American education is how little systematic attention is paid at any level to the process of planning and delivering these lessons to students in our schools. Within relatively broad curriculum guidelines, American teachers plan their own lessons on a daily basis. Moreover, they are expected, more often than not, to do it alone, without assistance from or consultation with their colleagues. There is little or no time in the daily routine of most American schools for serious discussion among teachers of what methods work best for helping children to understand a particular concept, nor do teachers have access to published lesson plans that have been systematically tested and shown to work. Inexperienced teachers typically receive no more assistance in meeting these expectations than teachers with many years of experience. Training programs for teachers in this country do not include extensive opportunities for supervised practice in school settings or for developing practical lesson plans for the specific situations in which they are likely to find themselves (because each school is different, and new teachers don't know where they will be teaching).

The result, once again, is that students are subject to the luck of the draw. Some get experienced teachers who have experimented with different methods and have learned by trial and error what seems to work best. Others draw inexperienced teachers who not only must spend a great deal of time figuring out what they are going to do every day but who also are likely to make many mistakes. Many end up in classrooms led by teachers who do not have the ability or the training needed to develop effective lessons. Even the best, most creative teachers, who are continually trying to improve their effectiveness as teachers, are certain to try approaches that don't work well for some or all of their students. Finally, it must be pointed out that inexperienced teachers and those who lack training are unequally distributed in our schools and school systems. For many reasons, including compensation and seniority rules, students who are most in need of good teachers are least likely to encounter them (National Research Council 2003).

The improvement of teaching methods, including their application in specific content areas, has been the focus of a great deal of research in this country over the last fifty years. Despite this investment, primarily by the federal government, the resulting research has been of very uneven quality and potential usefulness. Moreover, no one has been able to figure out a way to get potentially useful results into the hands of more than 3 million teachers in any systematic way. Finally, even if an effective distribution system could be imagined, there remains the question of when teachers would find the time to make use of it.

Textbooks

American beliefs about the importance of individual entrepreneurship also find their expression in another source of variability and therefore potential wasted effort in American education: namely, the textbooks used in our schools. In countries in which the national government exerts some influence over school curricula, the government also typically takes some interest in the content of children's textbooks. In Taiwan, for example, textbooks are written under the supervision of the Ministry of Education and uniformity in all schools is accomplished by providing a single textbook series for each subject (Stevenson and Stigler 1992). Other countries may not exert the same degree of control as Taiwan, but still insist that textbooks are consistent with national curriculum guidelines. In the United States, on the other hand, no coordinated effort is made to ensure that textbooks used in our schools cover the same subjects in the same way, or meet any particular standards. According to Stevenson and Stigler (1992),

The open market in the United States has resulted in a profusion of textbooks for every subject taught in school. The market is enormous, and both large and small publishing houses compete fiercely to get their textbooks adopted. There is no consistent system throughout the country for adopting textbooks. Some state governments exert control, but in other states the choice is left to local school districts, to individual schools, or even to the individual teacher. Because the content of the textbooks sometimes differs widely, the adoption of a new series is often a source of much controversy and wrangling by teachers, school boards, and state governments. (139)

The lack of any consistent system for deciding which textbooks will be used in the schools means that the textbooks actually used also can vary widely in their quality, thus adding to the uncertainty that surrounds the learning experiences our children encounter. Of course, the influence of textbooks on educational practices depends upon the extent to which teachers use them. This, too, varies widely from teacher to teacher, although few teachers feel compelled to cover all of the content contained in most textbooks. To the extent that different teachers cover different topics, it makes it very difficult for children's subsequent teachers to be sure what their children know and what they do not. Therefore, precious time and effort is sometimes expended by both children and teachers in repeating material that has already been covered and making up for material that should have been covered. This problem is compounded, of course, by the fact that many children in this country change schools and school systems frequently.

CONCLUSIONS

The cost of elementary and secondary education in the United States exceeds $350 billion annually, roughly 7 percent of the nation's gross national product. It is the principal activity of nearly 4 million teachers and administrators and more than 40 million students. It is a matter of great concern to the parents of these students, school board members, legislators and other government officials, prospective employers, including the U.S. military forces, as well as most other people in the country. Despite this huge investment of money, time, and effort on the part of such a large proportion of our population, remarkably little has been done to:

• apply in any systematic way what is known about the design of more effective learning tasks to what goes on in classrooms across the country,

- take advantage of the potential for economies of scale in virtually every aspect of our educational system; from teacher training to curriculum development to the preparation of teaching materials (including textbooks) to standard setting and the assessment of student performance, and
- make ongoing investments in research and development that are in any way commensurate with the magnitude of the enterprise as a whole.

Sustaining the engagement of learners depends in large part on their perception that they are, in fact, learning something. Both intrinsic and extrinsic rewards are linked, directly or indirectly, to the sense of accomplishment that comes with success in learning. Conversely, a perception on the part of the learner that his or her efforts are being wasted or are not yielding results is likely to have a negative effect on engagement in the learning process. Even when learners remain engaged, there is a great deal of room for improvement in the methods being used to teach American children and in the way schools are organized.

The central theme of this chapter is that the energies and effort of everyone involved in the nation's schools, including parents, teachers, and especially students, are scarce resources that should not be squandered as a result of inefficiencies in the way education is organized and conducted in this country. From inadequacies in the design of learning tasks in the classroom to inefficiencies in the way education systems are organized at the local and state levels, there is ample evidence that the country is not taking full advantage of the energies students, parents, and teachers bring to the educational process. Add to this the amount of effort on the part of teachers and other school personnel that is wasted because large numbers of students remain unengaged in learning, and the costs to society are staggering. These inefficiencies, moreover, are unequally distributed in society, to the detriment of low-income and minority students, particularly those living in large urban areas.

The bottom line is that the United States is getting a very low return on its investments in education, due largely to the lack of engagement of many of our students. No one could imagine a business enterprise comparable in size and scale to the U.S. education system that would or could tolerate the inefficiencies that contribute to this condition and that did not commit substantial resources to finding and implementing ways to improve its operations. Almost certainly, such a business would look first to standardize its operations and, in particular, to identify the most effective practices and procedures and then to ensure that they were implemented throughout the organization. Most major businesses, moreover, make substantial investments in research and development in an effort to continually improve productivity. The federal government provides almost three-quarters of the support for education research, yet this amounts to only about 1 percent of federal spending on education (National Research Council 1999a). State and local governments pay most of the costs of public schooling in the United States, but together make almost no investments in research and development.

The negative impact of underinvestment in research and development is compounded by the inability to take advantage of the results of the research that is supported. The decentralization of the education system as it is presently constituted and the lack of effective mechanisms for incorporating even the most robust research findings into more than a million classrooms makes systematic change very difficult, to say the least. The federal government tackled a similar problem early in the twentieth century when it created a system of land grant colleges, in part to generate knowledge that would help America's farmers increase their productivity. Responsibility for disseminating the new knowledge was given by the states to a corps of agricultural agents who carried news of the latest developments and provided support to farmers across the country in implementing the new techniques. It is worth seriously considering whether some variant on this model could turn out to be useful in the field of education.

Eliminating some of the inefficiencies in the way schools are operated would enable teachers to devote more time and energy to helping students who are having difficulties, rewarding students' efforts, involving students more actively in the learning process, and teaching students how to use their own energies more efficiently. There is good reason to believe that all of these things would help increase student engagement in learning. Finally, a focus on efficiency and effectiveness almost certainly would lead to a closer examination of the way time is used in the schools, with the result that interruptions and distractions to learning might be eliminated or at least reduced, and the amount of quality time spent on instruction in the core subjects increased.

6

VALUING EFFORT: SOCIAL AND CULTURAL INFLUENCES ON ACADEMIC MOTIVATION

For even the most able students, sustained success in school requires a great deal of hard work, perseverance, and self-discipline exerted over a long period of time. The preceding chapters of this book examined factors that influence students' willingness to engage in the learning process and to make the effort necessary to acquire skills and knowledge under specific conditions. These include learners' perceptions of their own abilities, expectations they have about their chances of success, rewards they receive for engaging in the learning process, and how learning tasks themselves are organized. Even to the most casual observer, however, it is apparent that there are very great differences in the attitudes and values regarding academic achievement with which different students approach school.

Some students come to school prepared to work hard and to do whatever it takes to succeed academically. During the time they spend in school, they continue to exert the effort necessary to respond to and often exceed the demands and expectations of their parents and teachers. Their commitment to academic achievement typically is relatively (although not completely) impervious to bad teaching, uninteresting subject matter, or distractions. Returning to the metaphor with which the discussion of engagement in learning began, these students' "engines are already running," and it is difficult to turn them off. In contrast, a great many students place a lower priority on academic achievement, essentially being content to do what is necessary to meet minimum requirements imposed by their teachers and schools. These students may become seriously engaged in learning when challenged or inspired by a particular teacher or intrigued by a particular subject, but these occasions tend to be the exceptions, not the rule. Finally, a smaller but significant number of students are not motivated to expend any effort at all on academic achievement in school. Their lack of interest in or motivation to engage in the tasks associated with acquiring academic skills may have characterized them from the beginning or it may result partly from their experiences in school, but it represents a formidable barrier to future academic achievement.

What are the sources of these predispositions to engage or not to engage in learning in school? What social and cultural influences help to shape and sustain children's attitudes and values toward school throughout their educational careers? What makes some children want to work hard, look forward to going to school, and take satisfaction from their accomplishments in school? Why do some children seem to have internalized the desire to succeed in school and to do what is necessary to succeed, with or without either encouragement or constant nagging by their parents or teachers? What forces, on the other hand, cause some children to devalue academic achievement and everything associated with it, including school?

It is clear parents, as well as many other adults in the lives of children, including their teachers, play a crucial role in instilling and sustaining the values of hard work, perseverance, self-discipline, and respect for authority that form the essential motivational underpinnings for academic achievement. Parents also play a special role in sustaining their children's motivation to succeed in school. Finally, American culture provides children and young people with a constant stream of messages, direct and indirect, about the importance of academic achievement and the role of our schools. This chapter is devoted to consideration of some of these social and cultural influences on children's attitudes and values towards academic achievement, including the important roles that significant others—especially parents and teachers—play in these processes, and the influence of cultural values more generally.

VALUING ACADEMIC ACHIEVEMENT—THE IMPORTANCE OF ROLE MODELS

The question of how children (or adults, for that matter) come to acquire what appear to be internalized, autonomous drives to succeed at something has been a subject of great debate within psychology for more than half a century. The phenomenon is of special interest because, among other things, it has enormous implications for schools. Children and young people who are highly motivated to engage in learning not only are a delight to teach but they have a great advantage over those students who appear to be less interested in academic achievement. Deborah Stipek notes, for example, that "students who value learning and doing well in school are more curious and mastery oriented, less angry and bored, more persistent, more likely to use learning strategies aimed at deep (rather than superficial) processing, and they achieve at a higher level than students who have not internalized academic values" (Stipek 2002, 142). Students who fall into the latter category require far more encouragement and attention on the part of parents and teachers to sustain their engagement in any learning task. If ways could be found to increase the number of students who are, in general, motivated to engage in learning in school, meeting the nation's goals for school improvement would be considerably easier.

Underlying many answers to the foregoing question is the idea exemplified in the apocryphal story concerning the rabbi of Kotzk:

> A townsman had requested that the Rabbi pray to insure that his sons would study the Torah diligently. In reply to the man's request, the Rabbi said: "If your sons will see that you are a diligent student, they will imitate you. But if you neglect your own studies, and merely wish your sons to study, the result will be that they will do likewise when they grow up; they will neglect the Torah themselves and desire that their sons do the studying." (Gewirtz 1969, 140)

This story captures a notion familiar to many parents. While direct training clearly is an important component of children's acquisition of behavior patterns, "by far the largest portion, and the most pervasive, significant, and long lasting of such patterns, is acquired through the active process of children's imitation of parent-models' behaviors" (Gewirtz 1969). Psychologists continue to disagree strongly about characteristics of mechanisms that facilitate the imitation and, more important, internalization of the behaviors of significant others—for example, the extent to which rewards and punishments are involved—but there is little doubt about the importance of role models in the socialization process (Piaget 1962; Miller and Dollard 1941; Bandura 1969, 1986; Pintrich and Schunk 1996).

In their major review of research and theory relevant to motivation in education, Pintrich and Schunk (1996) observe that

> People acquire knowledge, rules, skills, strategies, beliefs, and emotions by observing others. People also learn about the appropriateness of modeled actions by observing their consequences. From the time of the ancient Greeks, imitation has been postulated as an important influence on behavior. The Greek word *mimesis* (the root of imitation) refers to learning through observing the actions of others. (Rosenthal and Zimmerman 1978, in Pintrich and Schunk 1996, 157)

Over the last century, Pintrich and Schunk note, the psychological process involved in imitation has been conceptualized variously as the result of an individual's natural instincts (James 1890; McDougall 1926), as a developmental phenomenon by Piaget (1962), and as a product of behavioral conditioning (Skinner 1953).

Whatever assumptions one makes about the processes by which observations of another person's behavior are incorporated into one's own behavioral repertoire, several important observations can be made about role models and their relationship to learners. Many variables have been shown to affect the power of prospective role models to influence the behavior of individuals. Without doubt, the most important of these variables is the relationship of the model to the learner. For most children and young people, parents play a central role because of the special character of their relationship with their children. Especially the first several years of life, a child's dependency on his or her parents and the intimacy of the resulting relationship create strong tendencies to imitate parental behavior. Traditional personality theories attribute the strength of these imitative responses to the fact that such relationships are simultaneously nurturing and at the same time potentially threatening because of the child's dependence on them. Parents, therefore, serve as the prototype for a category of individuals called "significant others" who, by definition, exhibit these qualities of nurturance and threat of withdrawal of support. After one's parents, a variety of other individuals may function as significant others for any particular person— for example, members of one's extended family, siblings, teachers, and others who develop a relationship of special importance to the child, such as an athletic coach.

In addition to a model's relationship to a learner, several other characteristics of prospective role models have been demonstrated to have an important influence on learners. These characteristics include the model's perceived competence and status, similarity, credibility, and enthusiasm. As summarized by Pintrich and Schunk (1996, 167), "perceived model competence aids observational learning because students are more likely to attend to and pattern their actions after models who perform successfully than those less competent (Schunk 1987). Competent models also display skills correctly, which diminishes the likelihood that students will learn erroneously." Similarly, people tend to pattern their actions after people who possess high status.

Perceived similarity of models contributes to their effectiveness because similarity helps observers assess both the appropriateness of the model's behavior for themselves and the outcomes of that behavior. Similar models whose behavior is successful can increase learners' confidence that they can emulate the behavior, especially if models are seen as coping with the same kinds of concerns as the learner (Thelen, Fry, Fehrenback, and Frautschi 1979, in Pintrich and Schunk 1996). Models' credibility, as evidenced by the consistency with which they act under different circumstances, also positively increases their influence on observers' behavior. Finally, there is evidence that the enthusiasm with which models act can affect their influence on observers.

It is important to note that role models can have either a positive or negative affect on a student's attitudes and beliefs about academic achievement. Parents whose behavior reflects their antipathy toward schools or their view that academic achievement is unimportant or irrelevant for success in life are as likely to be imitated by their children as those who model positive attitudes and beliefs toward education.

Other adults in the lives of children—members of a child's extended family, teachers, and other individuals with whom the child has important relationships—also serve as models for the child's attitudes and beliefs about academic achievement, for better or worse, as do siblings and peers. Rarely do all of the significant others with whom a child comes in contact represent identical attitudes and beliefs, with the result that children often must choose, consciously or unconsciously, among conflicting values and behaviors to imitate and internalize.

SUSTAINING A FOCUS ON ACADEMIC ACHIEVEMENT

In addition to helping shape their children's attitudes and beliefs about the importance of academic achievement and learning, parents also play a special role in sustaining their motivation to succeed in school. Wagner (2002, 31) reports that "in a recent study of attitudes toward parental involvement in schools, 83 percent of the parents surveyed said that checking homework and encouraging kids to learn were their most important jobs in relation to school." The same study found, however, that an overwhelming majority of teachers do not feel that parents are doing these jobs very well. According to Wagner, more than 80 percent of teachers complained that parents of their students did not do an adequate job of setting limits for their children, controlling how much time they spent watching TV, or creating a structure at home that was conducive to learning. Eighty percent of teachers said that "parents' refusing to hold their children accountable for their behavior or academic performance" was a serious problem (Wagner 2002, 31). Remarkably, parents themselves agreed with their children's teachers; most admitted that they didn't know a lot about how to motivate their children.

These findings about the apparent ineffectiveness of many American parents in supporting their children's academic achievement are reflected in Stevenson and Stigler's (1992) observations about differences between the activities and perceptions of Asian and American parents with regard to school. According to these researchers, American parents place far more emphasis than Asian parents on preparing their children for entry into school, but pay less attention than their Asian counterparts to what is happening to their children once they begin school. Asian parents, in general, do not think that it is important to give their children a head start on the things they will learn in school. But once their children start school, "they regard doing well in school as the single most important task facing their children" (Stevenson and Stigler 1992, 93) and they expend considerable effort to provide support and encouragement for their children's schoolwork. In contrast, American parents are more likely to delegate more responsibility for academic work to their children's school while they seek to balance academic achievement with pursuit of other goals such as the development of social and physical skills (see chapter 7). The comparative data on early school achievement reveal the effects of these choices: American elementary school children start much faster than their Asian counterparts, but by the end of fourth grade their relative advantage has been erased.

The apparent disconnect between home and school in the United States is exacerbated by the fact that so much is happening in the daily lives of both children and their parents in this country. Not only is it the case that both parents work in a substantial proportion of families but parents and children are involved in an array of recreational and other activities that fill a large portion of available hours every day. These activities compete with school for the attention of children and parents alike, as we shall see in the following chapter. The result is a significant weakening of the most important source of ongoing support for attitudes and beliefs about the importance of academic achievement—parents.

THE ROLE OF CULTURE

As important as the role of parents and other adults is in shaping children's attitudes and beliefs about academic achievement, it is only part of the story. In addition to the individuals with whom a child interacts, every culture incorporates an array of models that exemplify the ideals held by the society and that help socialize children. As Stevenson and Stigler (1992) put it:

> Modeling is commonly used to shape human behavior. The idea is straightforward: Find people who exemplify the ideals held by the society and select aspects of their lives that can be described simply and dramatically. Keep the descriptions about each person consistent, and repeat the descriptions frequently, so that the characteristics of the models become

widely known. The models of course are much more complex human beings than they appear in the stories about them, but it is not the complexity of their lives that is important. They are selected because the culture
values the characteristics that they are reputed to display and encourages
young children to imitate them. (85)

Stevenson and Stigler note that in the past the United States has had
many well-known models—Benjamin Franklin, Abraham Lincoln,
George Washington, and, more recently, John Glenn and Martin Luther
King, Jr. who represented values and ideals every parent wanted their
children to internalize. Recently, however, America's cultural models have
more often been sports figures or entertainers than "heroes of service, science, or government," and rarely have they served as models of the attitudes and values associated with academic achievement. In fact, many of
the most popular figures on television consciously represent anti-intellectual values—consider, for example, the Simpsons. In contrast, other societies make much more deliberate and extensive use of models that por-
tray values that are regarded as important for children to learn: hard work,
perseverance, social and personal responsibility, and achievement.

A Japanese Role Model

Every school child in Japan nods knowingly when the name of Ninomiya
Kinjiro is mentioned. This youth, who lived in the Edo period nearly two
hundred years ago, was diligent in his efforts to learn. He was never without his books, and he used every possible moment to study, even while he
was helping his mother around the house or gathering firewood in the
forest. Statues of Kinjiro, with firewood on his back and a book in front
of him, may still be found in schoolyards throughout Japan. Recalling
Kinjiro's efforts, teachers and parents ask how students today, with so few
obstacles and such splendid opportunities, can have any valid reason for
shirking their studies.

Excerpt from H. W. Stevenson, and J. W. Stigler, *The Learning Gap: Why
Our Schools Are Failing and What We Can Learn from Japanese and
Chinese Education* (New York: Simon and Schuster, 1992), 86.

Overall, it is clear that American children are the recipients of mixed messages when it comes to the subject of the importance of academic achievement. As Paul Barton noted recently,

> Motivation comes from a myriad of messages a student receives—in the family, in the community, on the job, and in the culture—from the portrayal of learning in sitcoms to the ways students gain social acceptance from their peers. The hard fact is that mainstream American culture is not really a learning culture, at least not in the K–12 period of life. (Barton 2001, 14)

The recent influx of immigrants to this country from Asia and Latin America is having an important effect on American culture and the messages it incorporates about academic achievement. These effects are especially powerful in those parts of the country where large numbers of such immigrants have settled. Both Hispanic and Asian cultures stress the importance of family and the importance of family support for children's socialization. As has been noted, Asian immigrants bring with them an especially strong cultural commitment to academic achievement in school, which is reflected in evidence on the relative performance of Asian students in schools across the country.

One cultural value that has special relevance to learning in school is respect for others. It is clear that almost all learning depends upon the establishment of a relationship based on mutual respect between teacher and student, whether in school or out. As Wagner puts it, "as any good teacher will tell you, trust and respect are the foundation of active engagement and genuine learning in any classroom" (Wagner 2002, 29). On one hand, students must enter into such relationships with respect for the authority represented by the teacher's expertise and position. At the same time, teachers must respect their students and treat them accordingly. Over the last half century, however, beginning with the Civil Rights movement, there have been dramatic changes in the way Americans view authority (Wagner 2002). No longer are the opinions of people in positions of authority automatically accepted without question. The Civil Rights movement, the women's movement, Vietnam, and Watergate have provided numerous models of individuals who have questioned authority and the status quo. Young people have learned that questioning authority is appropriate and that people in positions of authority must earn the respect of those over whom they have authority.

Within the context of the school, these changes in society have profound implications, both positive and potentially negative. Few would argue that young people should not feel they can express disagreements with people in positions of authority, particularly when they are based on sound reasoning. Indeed, some of the most important role models that are held up to children as examples of America's best ideals— Martin Luther King, Jr., for instance—became heroes by standing up for what they believed to be true in the face of authority. At the same time, Americans want young people to know and behave in accordance with the principle that it is possible to disagree with someone and to respect them at the same time. A relationship based upon mutual respect also requires that both parties accord the other the courtesy of listening to and attempting to understand the other's perspective.

There is evidence that mutually respectful relations between teachers and students are becoming less common than they once were. Wagner reports a recent Public Agenda study that found that only 41 percent of all public high school students surveyed, across all racial and ethnic groups, felt that most of their teachers respected them. Moreover, "69 percent of the students surveyed said that they would learn 'a lot more' from a teacher who treats them with respect" (Wagner 2002, 29). While many young people complain about the way they are treated by teachers, teachers also complain that their students often do not respect their authority. The extent to which this represents a significant shift in the attitudes and beliefs of adolescents, who have always rebelled against authority, is unclear. From music to films to television, however, many of the products of the mass media aimed at the youth market espouse the twin themes of anger and defiance of authority. At the very least, American children and youth are bombarded with mixed messages about how they should view their teachers and other adults in positions of authority.

The cultural models to which today's young people are exposed take on greater significance, moreover, as the influence of parents and other important adults in the lives of children declines. Over the last half century, important changes have taken place in American society that have profound implications for the availability of adult role models that play such an important part in the transmission of societal values, especially the values of hard work and success in school.

THE ABSENCE OF ADULTS IN THE LIVES OF YOUNG PEOPLE

A number of scholars and others, from Urie Bronfenbrenner to Tony Wagner, have commented upon the fact that fewer adults play important roles in the lives of today's young people than was true fifty or even thirty years ago. The changes in society that are responsible for this fact are familiar to most of us. Perhaps most important, the number of single-parent and dual-career families has increased dramatically over the last several decades. Parents also are working longer hours and spending more time getting to and from work, with significant implications for the supervision children receive after school, as well as the amount of time parents have to assist with homework and other school-related activities. Changes in residential patterns, in particular the dramatic increase in the proportion of the population living in suburbs and increased residential migration, have decreased opportunities for children to have contact with members of their extended families or to develop meaningful relationships with storekeepers and other adults who live in their community.

One of the results of these changes in society is that young people are spending more time alone or in the company of friends, not with adults. A study of how adolescents spend their time conducted by Mihaly Csikszentmihalyi and Reed Larson (*Being Adolescent* (1984), reported in Wagner 2002) confirmed, for example, that

> Young people spent almost as much time alone, 27 percent of their week, as they did with friends, which was 29 percent. Only 5 percent of adolescents' time was spent with a parent or parents—and a disproportionate amount of that time was with their mothers. One-on-one contact with all other adults combined—teachers, a boss, grandparents, or other relatives—added up to only 1.6 percent of their time. (Wagner 2002, 34)

In his classic comparative study of Russian and American child-rearing practices, *Two Worlds of Childhood* (1970), Urie Bronfenbrenner called attention to significant cultural differences between the two societies in the importance each society attached to the upbringing of children. In the former Soviet Union, the raising of children was regarded as one of the highest priority activities for everyone in the society. Children were a primary focus of attention for almost everyone, and almost everyone felt a sense of responsibility for helping to ensure that children received both the care and attention necessary for them to learn important social values. Most children had a great deal of contact with adults outside of their own family and most adults participated in some fashion in the socialization of children and young people. According to Bronfenbrenner, for example, many work organizations, from factories to offices, established formal relationships with schools in which adults from the work organization participated actively in the lives of the school children. One of the explicit perceived responsibilities of adults outside the family was to support parents in caring for and socializing their children. One presumes that these cultural values and practices continue in today's Russia.

In this country, the burden of socializing children is borne primarily by parents and teachers, who themselves must balance many competing responsibilities. The result, as Wagner puts it, is that "young people today are growing up profoundly alone—perhaps more than at any time in human history" (Wagner 2002, 34). To an extraordinary extent, responsibility for the socialization of children has been delegated to the children themselves and to the mass media. It is not surprising, therefore, to discover that a substantial proportion of young people fail to develop commitments to the values underlying achievement in school.

INDIVIDUALISM VERSUS GROUP EFFORT

Another set of values that have an important impact on the way educational institutions function and on the relationship of students to them is the way a culture views the role of individuals, as opposed to groups, in society. A central tenet of American culture is the importance of the individual. American children are taught from an early age to be independent, to think for themselves, and to be responsible for their own accomplishments. This focus on the achievement of individuals is reinforced by competition among children beginning even before they enter school. Though many children participate in team sports, soccer, football, and Little League baseball, individual accomplishments are the focus of a great deal of attention; both children and parents are accustomed to making comparisons about the relative skills and accomplishments of particular individuals. Children also compete against each other as individuals in a variety of sports and other activities, as well as in school. Underlying all of these comparisons and competitions are cultural values regarding the importance of individual achievement.

Other societies place much greater value on the role of groups. In Asia, for example, an

> individual is typically defined through participation in groups—family, school, community, company, and nation. Primary obligations are to the group, and competition is between groups, not between individuals within groups. Individuals are aware of differences in the relative status of members of the group, but Asians minimize the significance of these differences in order to increase group cohesiveness. (Stevenson and Stigler 1992, 89)

From the standpoint of the school, group identification provides a powerful and effective means of increasing children's motivation toward particular goals. In particular, for instance, if group performance is rewarded more than the performance of individual members of the group, it does not take children long to figure out that they should do everything they can to contribute to the performance of the group. Often, this means helping the slowest members of the group because this is where the greatest leverage can be obtained in improving the group's overall performance (Bronfenbrenner 1970).

Increasing the status of groups relative to their members also makes it possible to enlist the support of groups in attaining the school's goals. As is discussed in greater detail in the next chapter, there is no doubt about the power of peer groups to motivate the behavior of their members. By rewarding the performance of groups in contrast to individuals in school, the power of the peer group can effectively be brought to bear on its individual members, thus co-opting the group in support of the school's goals. Finally, it is important to note that increasing the importance of group participation helps children learn how to cooperate with each other. The increasingly common practice of requiring team-based projects in American schools reflects our growing awareness of this fact.

As has been noted so often in the discussion of factors that influence student engagement and motivation, finding the right balance between opposing cultural values or beliefs about the nature of individuals is an important part of the problem. No one wants to trade American child-rearing practices that promote independence and self-sufficiency for too great an emphasis on the importance of group participation. Americans pay a price, however, for ignoring the potential power of groups to increase student motivation and engagement in learning and for underestimating the importance of skills that students acquire as a result of participation in group activities.

CONCLUSIONS

The attitudes and values regarding school and the importance of academic achievement that children bring with them to school reflect the influence of their parents and other important individuals in their lives and the diverse beliefs of the many different groups that make up the society. They also are influenced in important ways by American culture writ large, especially as represented in the mass media. Some children have internalized the idea that school is important and that they will be expected to work hard in order to succeed. Others bring more ambivalent or less well-formed beliefs about what will be expected of them in school and how they should respond. Many look forward to school as a social experience, an opportunity to spend time with friends. Some see school as an ordeal to be endured. To a greater or lesser extent, most children experience all of the foregoing feelings at one time or another.

These attitudes and values evolve over time as a result of each child's experiences in school, as well as the continuing influence of significant others, especially parents, and the culture at large. In some cases, parents continue to play a very significant role in actively supporting their child's engagement in learning; in many other cases, parents take a less active role. Barton (2001) concludes

Strong signals to achieve are necessary if we are to raise academic achievement in public schools. The signals young people get and respond to come from parents, peers, teachers, counselors, colleges, and employers. Teachers, who want the best for their students and who are being pushed by standards-based reform and accountability efforts to raise student achievement, deliver strong messages to try hard. But schools are not getting a lot of help from the other players in students' lives. They will not get far if they have to go it alone. (19)

The active involvement of parents in their children's schools declines as their children progress through the system, just as students' disengagement increases as they get older. There is some evidence that the more limited involvement of parents during the high school grades results in part from a cooperative process in which schools seek to keep parents at a little distance and students, entering early adolescence, are just as happy to keep their parents from interfering in their lives (White 2002). While some higher-income families continue to work hard to sustain the engagement of their children through high school, many minority and low-income families lack confidence that they can help their children during these years.

The increased demands placed on students by educational systems that are being pressured by society to enforce higher standards for all of their students seem certain to clash with these forces that lead to the disengagement of many students from middle school through high school. As Tomlinson put it so aptly in 1993, "After twenty-five years of trying to fix things, it is perhaps time to face a few facts of human nature: setting higher standards and expectations is one thing; persuading students to try harder is another. Educational reforms that do not change the study habits and behavior of students are unlikely to improve achievement" (11). Of crucial importance in making this happen is the sustained involvement of parents and other adults in the lives of young people through the high school years.

7

COMPETITION FOR EFFORT: ACADEMIC VERSUS OTHER GOALS

Adults frequently express wonderment at the seemingly boundless energy possessed by children. "Where do they get all that energy?" is a frequently asked question as children race from activity to activity throughout days filled from beginning to end with school, homework, play, extracurricular activities, music lessons, sports, computer games, television, and more. Periodically, someone persuades a professional athlete to try to do everything a twelve-year-old does during a normal day with the inevitable result that the athlete gives up, exhausted, long before the child shows signs of tiring. Regularly, stories appear about young people who manage to excel in school while simultaneously becoming accomplished musicians or athletes, or both. While ample evidence exists that children do, indeed, have a great deal of energy, probably more than most of the adults around them, this observation comes with two important caveats. First, just as is true with adults, there is great variation among children in their energy levels and therefore in the amount of effort any particular child can bring to any specific activity. And, more important, there are limits on the amount of effort any child can expend on any given day.

Limits impose choices. So long as opportunities to expend effort exceed the supply, it is necessary to decide how to apportion one's time and energies. Most children encounter more demands on their energies than they can satisfy and more opportunities to engage in activities that they want to expend energy on than they can manage. Another way to put this is that there is great competition for the scarce commodity that is our children's effort and attention. This book has focused primarily on characteristics of learning environments (and the contexts in which they exist) that have direct effects on students' engagement in the learning process. I turn now to consideration of the many things besides academics that compete for our children's energy, attention, and effort.

AMBIVALENCE ABOUT ACADEMIC ACHIEVEMENT

Despite strong evidence of the positive relationship between the amount of education children receive and their future earnings, and strong support for public education, Americans have always been ambivalent about schoolwork and the value of academic achievement in relation to other objectives for their children. Most parents want their children to be well adjusted socially, to participate in athletics, to develop leadership skills, and to have the opportunity to acquire artistic skills, such as the ability to play a musical instrument. Offered a choice between higher academic achievement and attainment of these other goals, I suspect that many parents would choose the latter and forgo the increased academic achievement, so long as their children were meeting minimal academic standards. As one would expect, students' views reflect those of their parents and the society at large with regard to the relative importance of academic accomplishment and other goals.

There are, of course, significant differences among different groups of parents and children in their views on these issues. Many parents and children are skeptical about their chances of success in school, irrespective of the amount of effort they are willing to invest. Others consciously place a higher value on forming a family or getting a job, or striving to achieve a nonacademic goal such as developing athletic or artistic skills. Some parents and their children, of course, believe that their primary focus should be on academic achievement. Even in these instances, however, they typically retain a strong belief in the importance of other kinds of accomplishments. These views are reinforced by admissions policies of even the most prestigious colleges and universities, which place significant weight on the record of a candidate's extracurricular activities.

The result is that people involved in the educational system—students, parents, teachers, and administrators, as well as those who help to make policy regarding schools—find themselves in conflict at one time or another about the amount of effort children should be exerting to achieve academic goals. On one hand, most Americans, including students, would agree with the statement that children could and should work harder in school. At the same time, most people are reluctant to change in any significant way the priorities they have established (consciously or unconsciously) about how they want their children to spend their time and energies.

These conflicting perspectives on the importance of academic achievement relative to other goals for children are consistent with the results of a survey of parent satisfaction with their children's performance in school conducted by Stevenson and Stigler (1992) as part of their comparative study of American and Asian education systems. More than 40 percent of American mothers responded to the survey by saying that they were "very satisfied" with how well their elementary schoolchildren were doing in school; in comparison, only 5 percent of mothers in Japan and China reported that they were "very satisfied" with their children's performance. The authors also found that

> American parents' high level of satisfaction was not limited to their children's performance. They also expressed high satisfaction with how well the elementary schools were educating their children. Among Minneapolis mothers, 91 percent said their children's school was doing a good or excellent job; only around 40 percent of the Sendai and Taipei mothers rated their children's schools as favorably. (115–16)

It is important to note that these findings do not reflect objective differences in how well students in the different countries actually were performing. Stevenson and Stigler go on to say that "These findings are particularly startling, given that these studies were conducted during a decade when great national attention was being directed to the weakened state of education in the United States" (116).

One explanation for these findings is that parents in China and Japan have higher standards for their children's academic achievement than do parents in this country.

> Education does not play as central a role in the American conception of the tasks and responsibilities of childhood as it does in Chinese and Japanese societies. According to most Asian parents, the major goal of childhood and adolescence is to obtain a good education, and families are dedicated to assisting their children in attaining this goal. (Stevenson and Stigler 1992, 126)

Put simply, academic achievement has a higher priority in Japan and China than it does in the United States. Another important reason is that, at least until recently, Americans have had very little information about how well their children are doing in comparison to international standards and what level of performance they should expect from their children. Even today, the reports that parents receive of their children's performance on standardized tests typically show how well they are doing in terms of national norms, not against objective performance standards.

The ambivalence Americans feel about the importance of academic activities is also reflected in the weak connections between the majority of parents and the schools their children attend in this country. While some parents play an active role in supporting their children's academic activities, including involvement with their children's schools, a significant proportion does not. For example, in 1996, only 22 percent of parents of children in grades 9 through 12 reported that they had been involved in three or more school activities in the last year. Thirty-nine percent of the parents of elementary school children reported similarly high involvement in their children's schools, but this percentage drops rapidly with decreases in mother's education and socioeconomic status (National Center for Education Statistics 1996a). Increased parental involvement in their children's education has been identified as a key element in every study of effective schools, yet it remains the most difficult of any of the objectives of school reform to achieve.

ACQUIRING NONACADEMIC SKILLS

Young people in all societies, but especially in this country, devote a great deal of time and energy to learning a variety of nonacademic skills. Most parents want their children to be "well rounded," a term that can mean a number of things, but usually suggests that their children have acquired knowledge and skills in several nonacademic areas—for instance, music, art, and athletics—as well as developed important interpersonal and social skills that are regarded as important for happiness and success in later life. No single set of skills meets the requirement for well roundedness; the important criteria are that young people achieve some level of proficiency in several different areas, according to their interests and abilities.

Schools participate in helping children achieve these goals by providing facilities, time, and instruction in many of the most important areas, and in particular, in music, art, and sports. They facilitate the development of skills in a variety of other areas through the mechanism of after-school clubs and activities and, in some cases, with formal instruction. Community-based groups provide opportunities for children, both boys and girls, almost everywhere in this country to learn and participate in a variety of organized sports activities, including soccer, Little League baseball, basketball, football, lacrosse, swimming, tennis, and even golf. The Boy Scouts, Girl Scouts, and 4-H Clubs offer opportunities for many children to learn a variety of other skills and to engage in activities, such as camping and hiking, that they might not otherwise have access to. Parents who have the necessary resources are likely to make sure that their children receive music or ballet lessons.

Detailed data on the amount of time and effort children spend engaged in such activities are difficult to come by. The National Center for Education Statistics summarized data from several sources on the participation of children of different ages in a variety of sports activities in 1994 (National Center for Education Statistics 1996b). These data show that 36 percent of all children ages twelve to seventeen reported playing basketball during the past year; 25 percent went camping; 23 percent played football; 19 percent played baseball; and 16 percent played soccer. Significant percentages of children also reported bicycle riding, fishing, swimming, playing volleyball, hiking, and running. Stevenson and Stigler (1992) report that the children they studied in Chicago spent on average four hours a week on sports. A quarter of all high school students report that they participate in after-school clubs and more than 14 million children participate in Scouting or 4-H Club activities each year.

For some children and young people, one or more of these activities becomes a major consumer of time and effort. Many children, for example, start out playing soccer or basketball or Little League baseball or participating on a swimming team when they are seven or eight years old. By the time they get to the end of elementary school, only a relatively small proportion of these children continues to be seriously engaged in organized competitive sports. For those who do continue, however, the demands on their time and energies can be very significant, in many cases several hours per day. The same pattern can be seen in other areas, such as music, where those children who pass a threshold of competence or interest and continue to participate in organized activities, such as the school band, chorus, or orchestra, are likely to spend a much greater amount of effort practicing and performing.

TELEVISION AND COMPUTERS

As every parent knows, television and computers, taken together, absorb a very significant portion of every child's attention on a daily basis. Numerous studies have shown that American children spend an average of fifteen hours a week watching television, as compared with about twenty-five hours a week in school. The average American child spends more than four-and-a-half hours a day in front of a television screen or computer monitor (Index of Leading Cultural Indicators 2001). One-fifth of all children and adolescents between the ages of eight and eighteen have a computer in their bedroom and, on a different survey, 57 percent of children aged eight to sixteen reported having a television set in their bedroom (Index of Leading Cultural Indicators 2001).

Both television and computers can and often do play a role in supporting academic achievement. Cable and satellite connections have dramatically increased the range of television programming available to many families, including a much richer menu of educational programs. Moreover, the number of U.S. homes with Internet access increased by more than 380 percent between 1995 and 1999 (Index of Leading Cultural Indicators 2001), and both schools and students are taking advantage of the opportunities this affords to expand the range of learning experiences available to many children. Finally, the growing presence of computers in homes and at school has enabled a steadily increasing proportion of students to become proficient in the use of computers. In all of these areas, television and computers compete for children's energy and effort while at the same time supporting academic goals.

Television and computers, however, have powerful entertainment value to children and most of the time they spend in front of a television or computer monitor is primarily recreational, not educational. The impact of this television watching, now supplemented by time spent playing video and computer games, has been the subject of much debate, most of which has focused on the content of the programs children watch or the games they play. Recent data indicate, for example, that parents are much more concerned about the content of television shows than they are about the amount of time children spend watching television (Index of Leading Cultural Indicators 2001). This finding is consistent with the report of the National Research Council's Committee on Developments in the Science of Learning (National Research Council 1999), which concluded

> In sum, television has an impact on children's learning that must be taken seriously. But the medium is neither inherently beneficial nor harmful. The content that students watch, and how they watch it, has important effects on what they learn. Especially significant is the fact that informative or educational programming has been shown to have beneficial effects on school achievement and that a preponderance of non-educational, entertainment viewing can have negative effects. Furthermore, the benefits of informative viewing occur despite the fact that the ratio of young children's viewing tends to be 7:1 in favor of entertainment television. These findings support the wisdom of continued attempts to develop and study television programs that can help students acquire the kinds of knowledge, skills and attitudes that support their learning in school. (National Research Council 1999, 139)

Irrespective of the content of television programs or video games, or the learning that may or may not occur as a result of watching or playing them, however, children's engagement in these activities absorbs enormous amounts of their time and energies. One can only imagine the achievement gains that might result if one could redirect toward schoolwork the energy expended during only one of the hours children spend in front of the computer or television set each day.

In this context, it is particularly interesting to note that Japanese children watch as much television each day as American children and that there appears to be little difference in the mix of entertainment versus educational programming watched by children in the two countries (Stevenson and Stigler 1992). The difference Stevenson and Stigler observed between Asian and American culture with respect to television viewing lay in the conditions parents imposed on television viewing. Chinese and Japanese parents were more likely than American parents to make television viewing dependent on the completion of homework. In seeking to explain the low achievement of American elementary school students as compared to children in Japan and China, the authors observe that it is not that Asian children play less than their American counterparts. They conclude that, "what does seem to be important is the way leisure time activities are managed. Chinese and Japanese children know that they will have free time only after they have completed the day's schoolwork. In American families, leisure activities and school compete for the child's time" (68).

Cultural differences between the United States and other countries in the extent to which parents play an active role in the management of their children's leisure time are underscored by data showing that, particularly for children over the age of ten, a very significant proportion of American children are essentially unsupervised during the period after school. Data published by the David and Lucile Packard Foundation suggest that as many as 30 percent of eleven- and twelve-year-olds regularly take care of themselves after school, while as many as 70 percent of those over the age of twelve are on their own at least some of the time (Kerrebrock and Lewit 1999). These data highlight the problem of not only the amount of effort that children are able to spend engaged in learning but how that effort is managed.

DEVELOPING SOCIAL RELATIONSHIPS

From the perspective of students, particularly adolescents, and often their parents as well, school is a place where young people learn much more than academic skills.

> It is a place to work on the broader "developmental agenda" of adolescence which includes adjusting to bodily changes precipitated by puberty, becoming more autonomous and self-directed, acquiring a sense of identity, making initial decisions about an occupation or career, committing to a set of values, and mastering new social skills—especially those related to romantic heterosexual relationships. (Brown 1993, 65)

From early stages of learning how to make friends in elementary school to acquiring much more sophisticated skills for coping with the complex social demands of adolescence, an increasing proportion of the energy and effort that children bring to school is directed toward forming and managing social relationships (Child Trends, 2003).

Although academic studies are the primary reason why children go to school, at least a third of students' time is spent in nonacademic environments: on the school bus, in the cafeteria or gymnasium, in the halls during class changes, in extracurricular activities, and before and after school. In addition, as everyone knows, down time in regular classes provides frequent opportunities for conversations about nonacademic subjects. When asked to specify the best thing about high school, far more students respond "being with my friends" than something about teachers, classes, learning, or achievement (Brown 1993; Everhart 1983). This is hardly surprising since, in the eyes of most adolescents, the most important things they are learning and experiencing during these years are related to social relationships, not academics. In the competition for students' attention and effort, therefore, the development and exercise of social skills takes center stage in the lives of a great many young people. Even those students who manage to sustain a focus on academics during the adolescent years often find themselves struggling to cope with the competing demands of their social environment.

Many, if not most, parents reinforce their children's natural inclination to be preoccupied with the development of social skills because they recognize the importance of these skills for their children's future success. They also want their children to enjoy life in addition to doing well in school, a perspective that is consistent with the value that Americans place on the importance of finding a balance between happiness and striving for success in life. Therefore, many parents encourage and facilitate their children's social activities in a variety of ways, from providing transportation to organizing social events, while attempting to help their children adjudicate among the many competing demands they face. Some parents respond to these pressures by attempting to place constraints on their children; others respond by essentially leaving their children to their own devices. Whatever their response, nearly all parents and teachers recognize that they are dealing with very powerful urges on the part of young people.

The Influence of Adolescent Peer Groups and Crowds

Since James Coleman published his classic study of adolescent peer groups in 1961, it has been widely acknowledged that peer groups play a very important role in the lives of young people in this country, including having significant influence on the motivation of young people to work hard in school. Coleman's findings suggested that many, if not most, adolescent peer groups reinforce anti-adult and therefore anti-intellectual values on the part of their members, essentially competing with school for the attention and engagement of their members (Coleman 1961). More recent work (Brown 1993) indicates that peer relationships among adolescents are a more complex phenomenon and that, in some instances, they may support academic achievement as opposed to undermining it. Clasen and Brown (1985) found, for example, that pressure to "finish high school" and "get good grades" were among the pressures from peers that were most frequently reported by adolescents. Consistent with Coleman's earlier findings, however, is their interpretation that this finding reflects a general peer norm that "encourages adolescents to do moderately well, to strive for academic adequacy rather than academic excellence" (Brown 1993).

Notwithstanding peer groups' direct influence on adolescents' inclination to engage seriously in academic activities, it is clear that membership in or identification with particular crowds or peer groups in school takes up a significant amount of the attention of most high school students. According to Brown (1993), crowds are a prominent feature of the social fabric of adolescence.

> In sum, crowds emerge in adolescence to help individuals master the developmental tasks of this stage of life, especially developing an autonomous sense of identity. They do not simply identify one prominent characteristic of a teenager but define in more comprehensive terms a lifestyle and value orientation. The diversity of crowds that one observes among teenagers underscores the fact that adolescents are not a homogeneous group. They confront the developmental tasks of adolescence in diverse ways, which are recognized as disparate lifestyles. The tendency of teenagers to routinely separate each other into crowds affirms the existence and importance of these disparate lifestyles and strategies of adaptation. (Brown 1993, 67)
>
> Some crowd labels are timeless. Groups such as the jocks, brains, populars, and nerds emerge in descriptions of the social world of high school that are written decades apart. Other crowd labels are time-bound— prototypic lifestyles that respond to the historical moment: greasers, rappers, skinheads, etc. The crowd label reflects especially salient characteristics of the prototypic lifestyle: intellectual competence (brain, "speds"), ethnic background (Asians, blacks, Mexicans), family socioeconomic status (richies, west-siders), a prominent activity or extracurricular pursuit (jocks, druggies, thrashers, "band fags"), social status or social skill (populars, nerds, snobs). Behind the label, however, is a much more extensive set of stereotypes that describe the group's hangout at school, academic orientation, typical weekend activities, involvement in illegal activities, orientation to others, and so on. Adolescents seem well aware of the crowds in their school. They can identify the stereotypic norms of each group and specify which of their peers belongs to each crowd. (Brown 1993, 65)

Not all students identify with a particular crowd or perceive themselves as belonging to a particular group (although there is evidence that most teenagers do, in fact, associate themselves with a particular group). Moreover, the specific effects any crowd or group may have on the academic motivation of its members or those who identify with it vary greatly. Some—for example, groups in which drug use plays a central role or those that ridicule academic effort—no doubt have a negative effect on the academic motivation of their members. Others may be organized around activities that can be a significant distraction from academic pursuits, such as the jocks or the socials. Finally, some crowds explicitly reinforce the academic orientation of those who identify with them.

It is also worth noting the potential of crowds and adolescent peer groups to create school environments that are so aversive to some teenagers that their motivation to go to school every day, much less to engage seriously in learning, is negatively affected. Since the tragic incident at Columbine High School, school systems across the country have been more aware of the potential effects of youth groups on individual students. Whatever their specific orientation or membership, however, the salience of crowds and associated peer groups in the lives of teenagers must be taken into account in thinking about strategies for increasing the engagement of students in learning.

Dating and Boy-Girl Relationships

Imbedded within the more general adolescent preoccupation with social relationships and the development of social skills is, of course, the matter of the inevitable physical attraction between boys and girls. In some other societies, dating is actively discouraged before young people complete secondary school (Stevenson and Stigler 1992). In this country, young people routinely begin dating early in their teens and, fueled by hormones and peer-group pressures, dating relationships between boys and girls compete strongly for a share of most young people's energies and attention. Good data do not exist on how much time adolescent boys and girls spend thinking about the opposite sex, but every indirect indicator suggests that it is a lot. Movies, television shows, magazines, and music aimed at teenagers reinforce their natural preoccupations with this subject.

Over the last several decades, as everyone knows, there has been a significant increase in the extent to which this interest in the opposite sex results in sexual activity among teenagers. In recent years, there has been a widespread perception that a majority of teenagers becomes sexually active at a relatively early age. Two recent surveys, for example, found that both adults and teens significantly "overestimated the percent of teens who were sexually experienced. Adults estimated that 69 percent of teens have had sex by age 15, and teens estimated 38 percent" (Child Trends 2001). However, data from the National Survey of Family Growth and the National Survey of Adolescent Males show that only about 25 percent of teens are actually sexually active by that age. "Moreover, [the data show that] not all sexually experienced teens are currently sexually active. While 50 percent of students in grades 9–12 reported ever having had sex (Youth Risk Behavior Survey 1999), only 36 percent of students had sexual intercourse in the past 3 months" (Child Trends 2001).

Data also show that the teen birth rate has declined steadily for all racial and ethnic groups since 1991. Due to the significant increase in the rate between 1986 and 1991, however, the current rate is still very close to the rate in 1986. In 2000, 157,661 babies were born to girls between the ages of fifteen and seventeen in this country, most of whom were unmarried (Child Trends 2001). Despite the recent declines in the teen birth rate, the U.S. rate is still one of the highest among all developed countries and is more that ten times the rate in Japan. Rates for Hispanic and non-Hispanic black teenagers continue to be nearly three times the rates of non-Hispanic whites in this country. The birth of a child is a very important event in any woman's life; for a high school student, it represents a major challenge to that student's ability to give attention and effort to schoolwork.

Whether teenagers' sexual activity results in a pregnancy or not, indeed, even if it only occurs in a young person's mind, it is very clear that attractions between boys and girls consume a disproportionate share of many adolescents' energies. As most adults remember, the emotions involved in the first relationships with someone of the opposite sex are powerful and often all-consuming, at least for some period of time. The importance of this fact for parents and schools, for how we structure learning environments, and for what we expect of our students is difficult to overestimate (Child Trends 2003).

EMPLOYMENT

A significant proportion of sixteen- and seventeen-year-olds work part time after school and on weekends. Statistics show that about 30 percent

of both young men and women still in school were employed part time
in 1993 and this percentage has remained more or less constant since
1970 (National Center for Education Statistics 1996a). No doubt reflecting the differential availability of jobs in different communities,
white males and females had significantly higher employment rates than
black males and females throughout the period. For those young people
who either choose to work for their own sake or who must work in order to supplement their family's income, there are potential educational
benefits, as well as liabilities. Work takes time and energy away from
other activities, including academic-related tasks. It can also be a source
of interpersonal and other skills that can be important for the future. In
any case, employment must be added to our long list of things that compete for the energies of many school-age youth.

OTHER FACTORS IN CHILDREN'S LIVES

In addition to the competition for attention and effort generated by
nonacademic activities, television and computers, developing social relationships, and employment, a very substantial group of children and
young people encounter demands on their energies that result from
other circumstances, many of which are essentially beyond their control.
These include poverty, unemployment, family instability or strife, neighborhood violence and crime, drug and alcohol use, and emotional and
health problems. In many instances, children must deal with more than
one of these problems in their daily lives due to the fact that they are
frequently interrelated. The negative effects of these problems obviously are disproportionately borne by children from low-income and minority families, but even children from the most affluent families are not
immune from the consequences of family instability or emotional or
health problems.

Poverty

Many children live in families whose financial resources are inadequate to provide the things that children need to function effectively in
school. In 1999, the federal poverty threshold for a family of three was

$13,861, and $16,895 for a family of four. By this definition, 19 percent of all children are growing up in poverty and 41 percent of children are living in families with incomes under 200 percent of the official poverty level (Larner, Behrman, Young, and Reich 2001; Phillips and Adams 2001). The poverty rate of children has remained essentially unchanged since 1980, while the proportion of children living in families with high income increased from 17 percent in 1980 to 25 percent in 1997. At the same time, the proportion of children living in extreme poverty increased from 7 to 8 percent. In 1997, 4 percent of children under age eighteen lived in households that experienced food insecurity with moderate or severe hunger (Forum on Child and Family Statistics 1999). Whether or not children in poor families have enough to eat, severe limitations on family resources have important negative effects on children's engagement in learning.

Unemployment

Inadequate family income is, of course, closely associated with the unemployment of family members. In addition to its obvious impact on financial resources, unemployment also has been shown to have other negative consequences for families and children. The stress associated with unemployment can result in changes in parenting styles and conflict between parents. These stresses, in turn, can result in increased delinquency and drug use on the part of adolescent boys and loss of self-confidence and depression on the part of girls. Younger children may be affected by more punitive disciplinary styles on the part of both mothers and fathers. Unemployment also may result in loss of housing, increased mobility, and, consequently, forced changes in schools for children (Rothstein 2002).

Family Instability

Income insecurity is much greater in one-parent families, and the percentage of children living with two parents declined from 77 percent in 1980 to 68 percent in 1996 and has remained stable since then (Forum on Child and Family Statistics 1999). In 1998, however, only 36 percent of African American children lived in two-parent families, compared with 64 percent of Hispanic children and 76 percent of white, non-Hispanic families. Single-parent families, of course, can result either from out-of-wedlock births or from the dissolution of two-parent families. As we have noted, the majority of births to teens occur outside of marriage (79 percent), but the majority of single-parent families result from the breakup of traditional two-parent families.

From the standpoint of children, while living in a single-parent family often presents challenges such as inadequate financial resources and greater stress on the single parent, the process of family dissolution (divorce or separation) can be even more distracting. As is by now common knowledge, the rate of divorce in the United States rose dramatically in the last half of the twentieth century and more than 50 percent of all marriages now end in divorce, affecting more than a million children annually (Shiono and Quinn 1994). Although remarriage rates have risen in recent years, more than half of the children in the United States will suffer through the divorce of their parents, in some cases more than once. Children in families whose parents divorce must not only cope with the fact of the divorce but usually must learn to live in a single-parent household, as well as deal with complex custody and visitation arrangements thereafter. Divorce often carries with it significant financial implications for parents and children. Even when marriages do not end in divorce, many children must deal with conflict within the family.

Arguments between spouses are one thing; domestic violence, often involving children as well as the adults in the family, is another. Although, once again, good data are difficult to obtain, social scientists estimate that between 3.3 million and 10 million children in the United States witness domestic violence each year (Osofsky 1999). It is also estimated that a very substantial proportion of men who batter their female partners also abuse their children. Data show that in 60 to 75 percent of families in which a woman is battered, children are also battered. There is evidence that children who witness violence, and especially those who are victims of violence, show symptoms of posttraumatic stress disorder similar to those of soldiers coming back from war (Osofsky 1999). As children get older, moreover, those who have been abused and neglected are more likely to perform poorly in school; to commit crimes; and to experience emotional problems, sexual problems, and alcohol/substance abuse. Clearly, such environments are not conducive to engagement in school learning.

Neighborhood Violence and Crime

In recent years, a growing number of children and young people live in neighborhoods that are characterized by high levels of violent crime, most of it associated either with drugs, youth gang activity, or, frequently, both. Often, these children also are exposed to violence within their own families, thus increasing the potential for serious psychological effects. As is the case with children who witness or experience violence in their own families, posttraumatic stress disorder symptoms of children living in "urban war zones" are similar to the symptoms of children living in actual war zones (Osofsky 1999). Studies of children living in violence-prone neighborhoods of New Haven, Chicago, Boston, Washington, D.C., and New Orleans found that a majority of children in each of these areas had been exposed to violence and, in many cases, had been a victim of violence. Virtually all of the children or parents surveyed in these communities knew someone who had been the victim of violence. It is impossible to imagine that these experiences do not have a significant negative effect on the ability of these children to focus on academic subjects in school.

Drug and Alcohol Use

Data from the National Institute on Drug Abuse's ongoing Monitoring the Future Survey (Johnston, O'Malley, and Bachman 2001) show that 54 percent of our young people have tried an illegal drug by the end of high school; 35 percent have tried such a drug by the end of eighth grade. The percentage of students reporting illegal drug use during the last thirty days increased dramatically between 1992 and 1999. For twelfth graders, the proportion rose from 14 percent to 26 percent; for tenth graders, 11 percent to 22 percent; and for eighth graders, it rose from 7 percent to 12 percent. Eighty percent of young people report having drunk alcohol by the end of high school; 51 percent have had a drink by the end of eighth grade. Remarkably, 64 percent of twelfth graders and nearly a quarter (23 percent) of eighth graders report having been drunk at least once. While there are some mildly encouraging trends in recent data, it is clear that drug and alcohol use among our children and young people continues to be widespread. Even assuming that frequent use of either drugs or alcohol is restricted to a much smaller proportion of the youth population, the impact of drug and alcohol use on the engagement of many young people in learning represents a major problem in our society.

Other Health and Developmental Problems

More than 10 percent of children between the ages of five and seventeen have serious long-term conditions or problems that interfere with or limit their ability to function in their families, school, or community activities (Forum on Child and Family Statistics 1999). In addition, health problems affect many students' ability to focus their energies on a periodic basis. Once again, poor children are more likely to be negatively affected by health problems ranging from asthma to lead poisoning than are middle-class children. For example, data show that poor children lose as many as 30 percent more days of school each year as a result of health-related problems than nonpoor children (Starfield 1997, in Rothstein 2002).

ORDER IN THE CLASSROOM—THE ISSUE OF DISCIPLINE

One of conclusions that may be drawn from the foregoing discussion is that competition for students' energies increases as they get older. Adolescence, in particular, opens up a whole array of possibilities and demands that clamor for students' attention on a daily basis. Moreover, this increased competition for the attention of students occurs just as they are expected to take more responsibility for their own behavior. These two themes in the development of young people present both families and schools with very substantial challenges. On one hand, everyone wants students to learn how to make choices for themselves about how they will invest their energies. On the other hand, our awareness of the many difficult choices confronting children leads to concerns that they will make poor decisions. We want our children to learn to manage their own lives, but we want to make sure that they make good decisions!

Acquiring the skills and dispositions necessary to take responsibility for one's own decisions and to understand the consequences of those decisions is, of course, a crucially important part of the socialization process for all young people. Clearly, both parents and schools play significant roles in this process, largely through the management styles they adopt for dealing with children under their control. Research on parenting has identified at least three different management styles: laissez-faire or permissive parenting, authoritarian parenting, and authoritative parenting (McCaslin and Good 1993; Baumrind 1971). Parents who adopt the permissive style "exercise little control and provide little instruction to their child." At the other end of the spectrum, authoritarian parents seek to "maintain control over their child's decision making and behavior irrespective of the child's emerging capacities. Authoritarian parents are less likely to discuss the reasons behind the rules. The goal is obedience, not understanding" (McCaslin and Good 1993, 254). Between these extremes, authoritative parents "provide explanations for their 'firm but flexible' limits on child behavior. They discuss their standards, teach their child how to meet them, and value behavior that is monitored by self-discipline and self-control" (254).

The work by Baumrind (1971) and others cited by McCaslin and Good (1993) provide clear evidence of the superiority of authoritative management styles, not only for parents but also for teachers.

> Authoritative methods . . . are more effective in building the cognitive structures and behavioral control mechanisms within children that enable them to become both independent and responsible in managing their affairs—self-regulated learners who can adapt to changing expectations. Authoritative teacher behavior should help students to understand and internalize the rationales that underlie classroom rules and to operate within the rules on their own initiative.
>
> Further, the nature of authoritative management recognizes the need for flexible rules so students can progressively assume more responsibility for self-management: a sort of instructional scaffolding in the interpersonal domain. . . . [In contrast], authoritarian approaches do not encourage the development of such internal control mechanisms, partly because they lack instructional components and do not recognize increasing competence of the learner. (254–55)

The implications of these findings for classroom management practices seem clear. As noted previously, a major goal of learning environments should be to move students from a focus on external rewards and punishments to the internalization of reasons for their attitudes and behavior. As children take on greater responsibility commensurate with development of more self-control, rules and structures must be adjusted accordingly. According to McCaslin and Good (1993), therefore, "teachers' behavior, rules, tasks, and expectations should change over time—within a school year and across grades" (255).

The importance of classroom management is underscored by a recent study of school connectedness—a student's feeling of being part of and cared for at school—utilizing data from the National Longitudinal Study of Adolescent Health (McNeely, Nonnemaker, and Blum 2002; Blum, McNeely, and Rinehart 2002). The study found that teenagers report substantially stronger feelings of connectedness when they attend schools that have more classrooms where students get along with each other and their teachers, pay attention, and hand in assignments on time. Smaller schools also appear to promote greater feelings of connectedness compared to larger schools.

Student behavior that is disruptive to the learning environment has always been a major problem for schools and individual teachers, but there is some evidence that such problems have increased in severity over the last decade. Data from the National Center for Education Statistics, for example, show that the percentage of principals reporting that student tardiness, tobacco use, absenteeism, drug use, and verbal abuse of teachers were serious or moderate problems in their schools increased significantly from 1990–1991 to 1996–1997. There is also evidence that such problems have a negative impact on student achievement (Barton, Coley, and Wenglisky 1998).

Despite these insights, relatively little systematic attention has been given to the relationship between classroom management styles and motivation of students to engage in learning in this country, particularly to changes in management styles that should occur as children advance through the grades in school. As noted in chapter 1, classroom management issues in this country have traditionally been approached from a disciplinary perspective, with the teacher as the central source of authority and enforcer of discipline in the classroom. Different management styles have been based on assumptions about what it takes to get different types of students first to behave appropriately in class and, second, to become engaged in learning. For those relatively few able, highly motivated, and engaged students, teachers can essentially put disciplinary issues aside and concentrate on figuring out how best to convey the knowledge, concepts, and intellectual tools that comprise the curriculum. For everyone else, the focus has been on what tools teachers have available to ensure compliance with the rules established by the teacher, as well as the school.

In the early grades, teachers in this country have always relied heavily on the use of rewards and punishment to motivate their pupils to behave well in class and to become engaged in the learning tasks. Before the turn of the century, corporal punishment was commonplace ("spare the rod and spoil the child") in school classrooms and teachers were likely to assume that "students were neither able nor willing to acquire the fundamentals of literacy without external compulsion" (Finkelstein 1989, quoted in Hampel 1993, 22). Even today, according to Webb, Covington, and Guthrie (1993):

Many proposals for motivating students seem driven by a belief that students are "obstinate beasts." Learning is seen as a neutral or even possibly an unpleasant activity, which is to be avoided if avoidance is possible. By this reckoning, learning will occur only as a consequence of the forceful imposition of positive and negative incentives in order to impel students to act against their natural inclinations. (100)

The most recent manifestation of this view of children, according to these writers, is the policy of intensification. This policy holds that "there is nothing wrong with our schools that cannot be remedied by doing more of the same—increasing the number of days in school, lengthening the school day, increasing homework assignments, raising standards, and setting higher requirements for graduation from high school" (Webb, Covington, and Guthrie 1993, 102).

At the same time, schools have become more heterogeneous and teachers have had to deal with students having a wider range of abilities, preparation, and commitment to school. The resulting cross-pressures on teachers have resulted in classes that are less authoritarian, as well as a "weakening of faculty power to enforce their notions of what was educationally desirable" (Hampel 1993, 26). A significant share of the burden for motivating academic performance has been shifted to students: "It's all here, but it's up to you to make the most of it." The erosion of older foundations of teacher authority also often leads to the negotiation of informal treaties with students, in which students acquiesce to teacher demands for order in the classroom in return for a lessening of academic requirements (Powell, Farrar, and Cohen 1985; McCaslin and Good 1993; Hampel 1993). At the middle and high school levels, the temptation to lower standards is reinforced by the perception held by many parents and teachers that teenagers should be allowed to indulge their preoccupation with activities associated with their physical, emotional, and social development, including organized sports, friendships, dating, and other activities.

This indulgence, or at least recognition of the importance of these activities that compete for our children's energies during adolescence, would have a less negative effect on many students' academic achievement if more students had internalized academic goals earlier in their school experience. In Asian classrooms, for example, children begin to take responsibility for their own behavior much earlier than do American children:

> A second factor contributing to the calm orderliness of the Asian classroom is that classroom discipline is not considered the responsibility of the teacher alone, but is shared with the children themselves. Children are given responsibilities for managing the classroom that far exceed those in most American elementary schools. The burden for maintaining discipline is shifted from the teacher to the children themselves, and especially to the child who is currently functioning as class leader. Because each child knows that he will eventually be responsible for maintaining class discipline, he is more ready to follow the suggestions of the day's leader. (Stevenson and Stigler 1992, 63)

An important goal for educational policy in the United States would appear to be finding a way to strike a balance between current relatively strict authoritarian approaches to classroom management and discipline in elementary schools and laissez-faire or treaty-based management at the high school level. Whatever balance is struck, it is crucially important that the impact of management practices on student engagement and motivation be given serious consideration. An overarching goal must be to get more students to internalize academic goals and the motivation to achieve them.

CONCLUSIONS: FINDING A BETTER BALANCE

The central message of A Nation at Risk and the most important theme of the two decades of school-reform efforts that followed its release is the need to strike a better balance between academic and nonacademic goals in American society. The principal methods that were proposed to accomplish this ambitious objective and that have underpinned the school-reform movement since then have included the establishment of higher academic standards for our schools and the implementation of more rigorous assessments of student performance in order to hold schools accountable for ensuring that all students meet the new standards. Placing all bets on the effectiveness of higher standards and accountability as levers to improve student performance seems overly optimistic, however, without taking more explicit account of the powerful forces that compete for our children's energies, most of which are not under the control of our schools.

Americans' ambivalence about the importance of academic achievement and the desire for our children to acquire a variety of nonacademic skills and abilities, together with our tolerance for and encouragement of the many powerful distractions to which our children are subject on a daily basis, raise questions about the extent to which higher standards, even when coupled with more rigorous assessments, can be successful in improving academic performance. If these sources of competition for children's energies are added to the continuing difficulties that beset a significant proportion of American families, the challenges that must be met in order to increase the engagement of many students in learning are formidable, indeed. At least as important is the fact that addressing many of these challenges is well beyond the purview of the schools. Awareness of the many sources of competition for effort, however, can lead to serious debate about goals for America's schools and schoolchildren.

In the context of the national focus on education and school reform, it would seem useful to find a variety of ways to stimulate a broader discussion about the importance of academic achievement for all students and what is meant by such achievement. Academic goals for all students must be seen as realistic, achievable, and compatible with other aspirations most people have for their children. They must also be linked more closely with labor force participation and the responsibilities of citizenship in the years ahead. The objective of such discussions, which must involve large numbers of parents who currently are only marginally involved with the schools, should be to reduce ambivalence about the importance of academic goals and shift the balance somewhat toward increased emphasis on student engagement in learning.

Assuming that any major reduction in the activities that compete for children's attention is unrealistic, attention should be focused on finding ways to manage such demands more effectively. This means, for example, doing things as simple as making watching television conditional upon completion of homework. Even such simple ideas, however, depend for their implementation on the determination of parents.

Ultimately, major increases in student engagement in learning at all levels depend on more students internalizing a sense of responsibility for their own learning and the management of their own effort. There are things that schools can do in the way classrooms are organized and managed, particularly in the early grades, to encourage the development of such skills and dispositions on the part of students.

Schools also can do more to reduce their complicity in the formation of treaties between students and teachers that have the effect of excusing students from engagement in learning in return for good behavior or making the lives of teachers and other school personnel more pleasant.

Finally, as a society, Americans must take seriously the fact that a substantial portion of the most severe problems faced by many of our schools are not caused by the schools, but rather by continuing crises in the lives of our students. The most significant factors in the lives of many students are those that result from inequities in our society and the social problems that result: poverty, unemployment, family instability, teenage pregnancy, crime and violence, and substance abuse. Although it has been said many times in the past, it is still unrealistic to expect schools to make up for such problems or to have much chance of engaging students who are expending most of their energies coping with the turmoil surrounding them.

8

ENGAGING MORE MINDS: INCREASING MOTIVATION AND LEARNING IN SCHOOL

The central thesis of this book, oft repeated in the preceding pages, is that engagement is a necessary condition for learning. Engagement in learning requires effort on the part of the learner. Increasing the amount of time students are engaged in learning, as well as the amount of effort they are prepared to devote to learning, therefore, are the keys to increasing academic achievement. In this context, I began this book with several observations about the extent to which elementary and secondary students in this country are engaged in the process of learning.

First, although the last two decades have produced a constant stream of calls for school reform and warnings that schools are failing to prepare children for the demands of the new economy, there is very good evidence that our best students are being served very well by the nation's schools. As many as 25 percent of students show every sign of being highly motivated to succeed in school and of being seriously engaged in the educational process. In return for their hard work in school, most of these students are benefiting from an increasingly rich and demanding array of education opportunities. It is, frankly, difficult to imagine what could be done to improve in any significant way the education most of these students are receiving in our public and private schools.

Second, despite the accomplishments of our best students, there is equally good evidence that a substantial proportion of young people—perhaps 50 percent—are far less engaged in the educational process, in general are not highly motivated to succeed in school, and are not working at anywhere near their capacity. This means that as many as 1.5 million students graduate from high school each year with only a portion of the knowledge and intellectual skills they need to participate fully as workers and citizens in our increasingly complex and technological society, not to mention the global economy. Remarkably, however, these students and their parents report being reasonably satisfied both with their schools and with their accomplishments in school. Neither the students nor their parents are clamoring for dramatic changes in their schools.

Third, a significant minority of students—as many as 25 percent—are essentially unengaged in the educational process and are not motivated to work hard, if at all, in school. These students score far below the best students and well below average on both national and international tests of proficiency in basic subjects, including reading, mathematics, and science. Many, though by no means all, of these students are from low-income and minority families and many attend large urban schools. Clearly, our educational system does not serve these students well. Moreover, despite almost forty years of federal and state assistance to schools that enroll a significant number of such students and isolated examples of successful reform programs, substantial improvements in academic achievement on any kind of scale so far have been extraordinarily difficult to come by.

Fourth, despite more than twenty-five years of intensive efforts by educators, researchers, policymakers, and politicians to find and implement ways of improving schools, including the investment of substantial public and private resources, there has been little or no measurable effect on the output of the nation's school systems. While the achievement gap between minority and nonminority students has declined somewhat in some fields, wide disparities between these groups remain and there has been little change in overall scores on most measures of academic achievement.

Finally, this inability to achieve significant improvements in the performance of schools is truly remarkable in light of the enormous potential for improvement represented by the fact that so many American schoolchildren spend so little time and effort engaged in academic learning. As long as such a significant proportion of students are either indifferent to school or alienated from it, it is not surprising that efforts at school reform have not yielded greater results. Yet if ways could be found to increase the engagement of the vast majority of students in learning—even by a modest amount—the results would be dramatic, indeed.

A PRIMARY FOCUS ON STUDENT ENGAGEMENT

These observations lead to a focus on the processes by which students become engaged in learning and the factors that influence the amount of effort they are prepared to invest in learning once they have become engaged, particularly (though not exclusively) in school. One of the most important conclusions that emerges from this analysis is that a great many things can and often do influence the inclination of students to engage in learning, both in general and in the context of any particular learning task. These influences, moreover, often are related to one another in complex ways, making the task of thinking about how to intervene in the process more difficult.

Although conceptually it is necessary to take into account the interrelationships among all of the relevant factors in analyzing student engagement in learning, one can distinguish five key barriers to student engagement in the nation's schools.

- Beliefs about the relative importance of ability versus effort in learning and perceptions of one's own abilities.
- The relative scarcity of rewards for learning.
- The extraordinary inefficiencies in the way education is organized and conducted in this country.
- The ambivalence about the value of academic achievement and the importance of hard work in school that is inherent in American culture.
- The fierce competition that occurs for the effort and energy of students between academic obligations and many other activities and demands.

BARRIER #1: EFFORT VERSUS ABILITY IN LEARNING

A learner's beliefs about the relative importance of effort versus ability in learning, coupled with an assessment of his or her own abilities, plays a crucial role in the learner's willingness to engage in any learning task and to exert, over time, the effort necessary to succeed at that task. The sources of an individual's beliefs, both about the importance of innate abilities for learning and about his or her capabilities are complex, but all of them are shaped by the views of society on these issues.

While there is much talk in American society about the importance of hard work and its relationship to success in life, most Americans act as though innate abilities are the primary determinants of their most important accomplishments. Americans have been fascinated by the notion of inherited aptitudes and abilities for more than a hundred years; throughout this period, schools have reflected this preoccupation with native ability. The result, as Resnick recently pointed out, is that "schools largely function as if we believed that native ability is the primary determinant in learning, that the 'bell curve' of intelligence is a natural phenomenon that [is] reproduced in all learning, and that effort counts for little" (Resnick 1995, 56). These beliefs are reflected in a variety of educational policies and practices. These include the use of measures of intelligence to select students for gifted and talented programs, scoring of standardized achievement tests based on comparisons with how well other students perform as opposed to independent standards, grouping of students by ability for instructional purposes in many classrooms, and the continued reliance on college admissions tests that purportedly measure aptitudes instead of achievement.

Resnick goes on to point out that these policies and practices represent "institutionalized expressions of a belief in the importance of aptitude . . . that are far more powerful than what we might *say* about the importance of effort" (57). Most parents, teachers, and students themselves accept the view that aptitude and innate abilities matter greatly. For many students, the result inevitably is diminished motivation to work hard in school, based on the assumption that they do not have the necessary abilities to succeed. Even for those students who have a strong positive assessment of their own abilities, stress on the importance of these abilities can negatively affect their willingness to make mistakes in learning, because mistakes often are assumed to reflect lack of ability.

It is unrealistic and perhaps unwise to suggest that schools attempt to ignore the role played by aptitudes and abilities in learning and academic achievement. Clearly, there are many instances in which especially able children need special opportunities in order to realize their potential, just as there are children at the other end of the spectrum of ability who can benefit from special attention and programs designed to meet their needs. It is, however, reasonable to urge the reexamination of a number of policies and practices that put undue emphasis on innate abilities more broadly and, in particular, have the potential to diminish the motivation of many students who are perfectly capable of succeeding in the educational system.

Essential to an educational system that places greater emphasis on student effort are clear expectations for what students are expected to accomplish, and equally clear measures of their progress toward achieving those goals. As Resnick puts it, "If students are to work hard, they need to know what they are aiming for" (58). In addition, they must know what criteria will be used for judging whether or not they meet these standards. Especially important is the expectation that all students can and should meet the standards. Recent emphasis on the establishment of rigorous standards for student achievement, coupled with performance-based measures of progress in meeting these standards, is consistent with this requirement. Thus far, however, with the exception of the development of high school exit examinations in some states, most of the attention devoted to the development of standards and accountability has been focused on measures of the performance of schools or school systems, not individual students. Both students and their parents must be given regular and meaningful feedback on their progress toward meeting explicit performance goals.

In setting standards and raising expectations for student performance, it is also important to make sure that as many students as possible have the experience of succeeding at *something*. Howard Gardner's (1991) work on multiple intelligences suggests strongly that in developing both standards and measures of performance, ways are found to take account of differences in interests and types of abilities among students. The new economy, moreover, requires a much broader range of skills and intellectual abilities than most schools are accustomed to providing. The Secretary of Labor's Commission on Achieving Necessary Skills (SCANS) (U.S. Department of Labor 1991), for example, generated a list of some twenty-eight skills that all adults should have in order to participate effectively in America's rapidly changing society, as well as the global economy. The commission proposed creation of a certification system that would enable students to demonstrate their proficiency in each of these skills at any time during their school career, in the same manner that Scouts accumulate merit badges based on their interests and abilities. These ideas suggest strongly the need for development of a range of new measures of students' skills and abilities that would, among other things, enable more students to demonstrate the result of their efforts. An important implication of this point is that some of the efforts currently being devoted to creating "better" measures of student achievement should be redirected to developing new measures of different skills and abilities.

Both the SCANS Commission recommendations and the merit badge concept underscore the importance of finding find new ways to give students both the time and the support they need to develop particular skills and areas of knowledge. Increased flexibility on the part of schools would allow students to proceed at different rates in accordance with their abilities, but with the expectation that all students can and should reach high minimum standards of accomplishment. As everyone knows, however, flexibility in scheduling and in the deployment of instructional resources are among the most difficult things for schools to do. Figuring out how to accomplish this objective will take real creativity and almost certainly require the resources of institutions that are not now formally part of our educational system: for example, churches, settlement houses, the Scouts, 4-H Clubs, and other youth service organizations (Resnick 1995, 60).

BARRIER #2: REWARDS FOR ENGAGEMENT IN LEARNING

Rewards play an essential part in getting students engaged in the learning process in the beginning and in sustaining their engagement and motivation to learn over time. Some rewards appear to be intrinsic to the learning task—that is, the task itself is inherently interesting or enjoyable. Others are independent of the task—for example, attention, encouragement, or praise from parents or teachers. If it were possible to make all learning tasks intrinsically rewarding to all learners all of the time, there would be no need for school reform or, for that matter, this book. Sustaining the engagement and motivation of learners over time, however, no matter how interesting or enjoyable the particular task may be at the outset, almost always depends upon the availability of extrinsic rewards. This is because a great deal of learning involves hard work on the part of the learner. As learners gain in feelings of competence and control over the learning task, extrinsic rewards may decline in importance (becoming an expert in something seems to be intrinsically rewarding). Most learning, however, depends upon at least an occasional extrinsic reward to sustain any learner's engagement and motivation.

The availability of rewards for engagement and learning in school is problematic on two grounds. First, there is abundant evidence that the vast majority of learning tasks are not intrinsically interesting or engaging, at any time. Despite pleas from students, parents, and educators themselves for curricular materials that are more interesting, that enable students to become more actively involved in the learning process, and that lead more quickly to a sense of mastery on the part of students, much of what students encounter in school does not meet any of these criteria. In part, this is due to a failure of the education industry as a whole (a point to which I will return below). In part, it results from the fact that there are many who argue that school curricula should *not* be intrinsically interesting. According to this view, it is important for students to understand that not all learning is or can be fun and that part of the educational process itself is to learn to sustain one's effort even when the material is drudgery. Not very long ago, many college-bound students were required to learn Latin, in large part because of the discipline required to master it.

The second problem faced by schools is the fact that there are not enough extrinsic rewards available to sustain the motivation and engagement of all students. The first and most important reason for this shortage is the ratio of potential reward givers—that is, teachers—to students.

Particularly at the middle and high school levels, where most teachers are responsible for the instruction of more than one hundred students on a daily basis, it is simply not possible for teachers to pay attention to and provide encouragement to all of their students on any regular basis. A second reason is that most schools are organized in accordance with a system of scarce rewards. In many, if not most, classrooms across the country, teachers grade on a curve; that is, only so many As and Bs are awarded in each class, irrespective of the performance of the rest of the students in the class. Underlying this practice is the philosophy that if all of the children received high marks, grades would lose their value to motivate student performance. The result, therefore, is that many students are not motivated to work hard because they know that they have little chance of beating out the best students for a good grade.

The best and most highly motivated and engaged students, of course, absorb the lion's share of the scarce extrinsic rewards that schools have available: they receive most of the attention and encouragement teachers are able to dispense and they account for most, if not all, of the good grades. It is not surprising, therefore, that the best students do very well and that the majority of students in most schools are less engaged in learning, if they are at all. What might be done to address this problem?

First, more attention should be devoted to the problem of making what happens in our schools more intrinsically rewarding and therefore engaging to students. The complexity of the processes of generating and sustaining student engagement in most learning tasks suggests that much more should be done to help teachers select and use proven instructional tools and techniques that will engage more students. In many other countries, teachers work hard to craft lessons and to deliver them in the most effective manner. Nothing even close to this practice occurs in the vast majority of American schools and classrooms.

Second, many students come to school with preconceptions about whether certain subjects—mathematics, for example—are boring or difficult. Many of these preconceptions turn out to be self-fulfilling prophecies; that is, student expectations help make them come true. In other cases, teachers reinforce the preconceptions through the way in which they present material. Again, studies of schools in other countries demonstrate that many such subjects can be presented in ways that will engage the interest of students.

Third, while there is no question that intrinsic motivation is desirable, one message that emerges clearly from the analysis in this book is that ways must be found to increase the availability of extrinsic rewards for engagement in learning. One way to do this is to increase the number of reward-givers in schools, notwithstanding the budgetary constraints every school faces. Obviously, it would be a good thing if teachers were responsible for teaching fewer students on a regular basis and therefore had more time to pay attention to each one. Other adults—teacher aides, volunteers, senior citizens—could augment the attention teachers are able to give students, particularly if they were assigned to help those students who need encouragement the most. Programs in some schools have demonstrated that older students also can serve as an important source of encouragement and attention for younger students without negative effects on their own learning. Overall, the basic principle is to get more people to pay attention to our students.

Fourth, in this vein, a number of reformers recently have urged that the size of schools be reduced significantly, with the goal of creating more personalized learning communities and thereby increasing the chances that every student will have someone who cares about him or her. The Bill and Melinda Gates Foundation is making significant investments to encourage the formation of smaller schools and this idea is at the center of Tony Wagner's book *Making the Grade* (2002).

Fifth, a focus on the importance of extrinsic rewards also suggests that alternatives are needed to the widespread practice of awarding grades based on the relative performance of students in a classroom, in contrast to their performance measured against objective standards. Providing students with clear information about what they are expected to learn and then awarding grades based on whether they meet such standards, irrespective of how they do relative to other students in the class, could have the effect of substantially increasing the availability of rewards. With higher standards, clearer expectations for what students are expected to learn, more flexibility with regard to the amount of time students have to learn, and good measures of student performance, it should be possible for many more students in a classroom to receive high grades without devaluing the currency. The challenge for teachers remains the same as always: to set high standards for their students' performance and then to make sure every student succeeds.

Finally, experiments should be undertaken with alternative reward structures, such as assigning grades based on the performance of groups of students. If each member of a group composed of students of different levels of ability (or motivation) received the same grade, based on the average scores of the members, it would clearly be to the advantage of the most able members of the group to help the weakest members.

BARRIER #3: INEFFICIENCIES IN LEARNING PROCESSES

The effort that students invest in learning must be viewed as a scarce commodity. The amount of energy each student has to invest in learning anything is limited; students can ill afford to squander it on learning strategies that are either inefficient or ineffective. This is one of the reasons parents look for good teachers and schools for their children, not to mention for themselves when they want to learn a new skill, be it how to use a computer or play golf. It is in everyone's interest to make sure that learning occurs as quickly and as efficiently as possible. When someone perceives that he or she is not getting a reasonable return on his or her investment in learning, he or she is likely to reduce the investment or eliminate it altogether. When this happens, effort invested up to that point may be wasted, subsequent learning may be impaired, and the individual's willingness to engage in learning in the future may also be negatively affected.

There is a great deal of evidence that an enormous amount of effort on the part of children, not to mention their parents and teachers, is wasted as a result of inefficiencies in the way teaching and learning are organized and conducted in our schools. The sources of these inefficiencies include inadequacies in the design of learning tasks, the inability of students to manage the investment of their own effort in learning, the way learning environments are organized in schools, and how the educational enterprise as a whole is organized and managed in this country.

With regard to the design of learning tasks, much has been learned in recent years about the importance of the "fit" between characteristics of the learner and the learning task, including the preconceptions learners bring with them to the task. More is also known about how to help learners cope with difficulties they encounter as they engage in learning and about the importance of enabling learners to play a more active role in the learning process. Everyone has become more conscious of how important it is for learners to receive frequent feedback on their performance. Finally, observations of schools in other societies have shown that many devote more attention to explicit teaching of methods that students can use to increase the efficiency of their own learning, including retention techniques, study aids, and strategies for managing their own time and efforts.

How learning is organized in American classrooms also affords many opportunities for increasing the efficiency and effectiveness of learning and teaching on the part of students and teachers. There is clear evidence based on observations of schools and classrooms in other countries that students could and should take much more responsibility for, as well as a more active part in, their own learning than is typically the case in most American schools. How much and what types of learning we expect of our students warrants reexamination, as does the extent to which different parts of the learning environment fit together and reinforce one another. Finally, the amount of time actually spent on learning in American classrooms deserves serious attention, along with the way that time is structured.

Underlying all of the foregoing observations about sources of inefficiencies in how learning and teaching are organized and conducted in our schools is a set of broader issues stemming from the way Americans view their schools and how they should be managed. Central to these views are beliefs in the importance and uniqueness of individuals and in the principle of local control of our schools. The first of these beliefs leads to the principle that the instruction each child receives should be designed specifically for his or her abilities and needs. The second leads to the automatic rejection of proposals for everything from a common curriculum and assessments to uniform approaches to teaching.

Adherence to these principles, however, carries with it very high costs to society. Insistence upon a model of individualized instruction, however unrealistic and unachievable, almost certainly increases inequities in the attention individual students receive, while adding to the burden of already overworked teachers. Insistence upon the principle of local control makes it more difficult for schools to take advantage of increases in knowledge about the most effective methods of teaching or to benefit from economies of scale in the development and implementation of curricula or assessments of student performance. Expecting each teacher in each school to develop methods for teaching his or her own version of the local curriculum wastes an enormous amount of every teacher's precious time and energies, and produces, at best, instruction of mediocre and inconsistent quality. Finally, insistence on decentralization and individualization of the educational process makes it more difficult for teachers to find the time to do what they are supposed to be doing: namely, teaching their students (not to mention providing students with the rewards they need to sustain their engagement).

These observations lead to the following conclusions and suggestions for educational policy and practice. First, it is time for a serious national dialog about the costs and benefits of increased uniformity of curricula and teaching methods in the United States. A high price is being paid for gross inefficiencies in the way our schools are organized and operated. It may be possible to find ways of maintaining local control over things that matter most to parents while realizing very substantial gains in the efficiency and effectiveness of our educational systems through economies of scale and more widespread adoption of best practices. I suspect that most parents, teachers, and school administrators would readily trade some of what may, in fact, turn out to be largely illusory control of their local schools in return for more effective teaching materials, better assessment tools, more time for teachers to prepare lessons and work with students, and more resources to invest in their schools.

Second, finding ways to encourage schools to adopt curricula and teaching methods that have been proven to be effective assumes that we know what curriculum materials and teaching methods are, in fact, most effective under a range of different circumstances. Although some progress has been made in understanding what works best, the nation is still underinvesting by a significant margin in the research and development necessary to support the development and increased utilization of best practices in our schools.

Third, although knowledge about the most effective approaches to teaching and learning continues to grow, it is also important to experiment with new ways of disseminating this knowledge to teachers, schools, and school systems. Among the approaches that deserve consideration is establishment of a state-supported and managed corps of "educational agents," patterned after the system of agricultural agents that provided scientifically based information and assistance to farmers during the first half of the last century. An important opportunity exists to learn from both the mistakes and accomplishments of the agricultural agent program and to determine whether it is possible to adapt this model to our highly decentralized education system.

Fourth, it is particularly important to make it possible for teachers to devote more systematic attention to planning and delivering lessons to their students. As has been noted above, most American teachers plan their own lessons, alone, on a daily basis. There is little or no time in the daily routine of most schools for serious discussion among teachers of what methods work best for helping children understand a particular concept, nor do teachers have access to published lesson plans that have been carefully tested and shown to work. Inexperienced teachers typically receive no more assistance in meeting these expectations than teachers with extensive experience. In every other field of endeavor that requires expert performance and where high stakes are associated with the outcome, participants are expected to practice their skills or rehearse their performance before going on stage. The same should be true for teachers.

Fifth, part of a national dialog on the costs and benefits of increased standardization of curricula and teaching practices should be devoted to an examination of textbooks in American schools. It is inconceivable that all of the different textbooks that find their way into our schools are really needed, that all of them are equally effective, or that any given school board or committee of parents and teachers is really qualified to determine which book will be the most effective. As everyone knows, the Food and Drug Administration requires extensive scientific testing of both efficacy and safety before any new drug can enter the market. Are children's textbooks any less important or potentially harmful?

Sixth, the report of the National Education Commission on Time and Learning (1994) documented very significant inefficiencies resulting from the way time is used by students and teachers in schools. Among the commission's major recommendations were the need for increased flexibility in order to enable students and teachers to pursue topics that don't fit neatly into a fifty-one-minute period, the elimination of distractions and interruptions during instruction periods, and adaptation of schedules to accommodate the needs of students of varying levels of ability. These and other recommendations of the commission deserve very serious consideration.

Finally, a portion of the curriculum at every grade level should be devoted to teaching students how to use their energy and effort more effectively. Ample evidence exists that this is done routinely in many other countries to good effect. Increased time and energy management skills are especially important for American children to have, given the competing demands on their time.

BARRIER #4: AMBIVALENCE ABOUT THE VALUE OF ACADEMIC ACHIEVEMENT

Significant differences exist among students in the degree to which they value academic achievement and are inclined to work hard in school. Some students come to school prepared to work hard and to do whatever it takes to succeed academically. Other students place a lower priority on academic achievement and, unless engaged by a particular teacher or an interesting subject, are content to do what they need to do to meet minimum requirements. The occasions on which they become seriously engaged in learning tend to be the exception rather than the rule. Finally, some students are disinclined to invest any effort at all on academic achievement in school. For such students, their lack of interest or motivation to engage in learning presents a formidable barrier to their acquiring many of the skills they need to participate fully in society.

The sources of the values children bring with them to school include their parents, other adults who play significant roles in their lives, their peers, and a variety of role models, both fictional and real, produced by the culture in which they live. Parents play an especially important role in instilling and sustaining the values of hard work, perseverance, self-discipline, and respect for authority that form the essential motivational underpinnings for academic achievement. While attention is usually focused on the positive role parents and other adults play in nurturing and sustaining academic motivation, it should be noted that these powerful influences on students can be negative as well as positive. Students' values and motivation to engage in learning are also influenced, both positively and negatively, by the constant stream of cultural messages they receive on a daily basis, principally from the mass media.

If one looks carefully at the sources of children's beliefs and values regarding the importance of academic achievement in American society, one thing stands out clearly: most children are the recipients of mixed messages. Some children's parents place high priority on academic achievement and devote considerable effort to instilling in their children the values of hard work, perseverance, self-discipline, and respect for authority needed for success in school. Many such parents continue to reinforce these values throughout their children's experiences in school. Others convey feelings of ambivalence or even skepticism about the importance of achievement in school, placing higher priority on other goals for the children, such as the development of social skills or athletic abilities. Whatever children acquire from their parents, they are certain to encounter models that represent different values, including among their peers and in the culture at large.

The inconsistency that many, if not most, students encounter in beliefs about the importance of academic achievement cannot help but affect their inclination to engage seriously in learning in school. As has been noted, some students enter school and remain committed to academic achievement and to investing the energy necessary to meet and exceed the demands and expectations of their parents and teachers. The attitudes of the majority of students, however, reflect the society's ambivalence about the importance of academic achievement and these students remain only marginally engaged in the learning process.

Changing this state of affairs will not be easy because America's diverse and democratic society offers few, if any, efficient mechanisms for modifying public opinion on any kind of scale. In a few areas, however, there has been substantial change in both the attitudes and behavior of a significant proportion of the population over the last two or three decades. The implications of these examples for what might be done to increase the importance society attaches to academic achievement will be addressed in the concluding section of this chapter.

BARRIER #5: COMPETING DEMANDS FOR STUDENT EFFORT

The ambivalence many students and their parents may feel about the importance of academic achievement at once reflects and is compounded by the many competing demands on the energies of children. These demands include (1) the expectation that children will acquire one or more nonacademic skills—for example, in music, the arts, or athletics; (2) the substantial amount of time virtually every child devotes to television and, more recently, computers; (3) the development of social skills and relationships; (4) the claims that peer groups and "crowds" in school make on both the time and attitudes toward school of many students; (5) dating and experimentation with important personal relationships; and (6) employment after school and on weekends. In addition, it was noted that for significant subsets of the student population, a variety of other problems serve as major impediments to engagement in learning academic skills. These include poverty, family instability, inadequate housing, violence and crime in their communities, substance abuse, and health or developmental problems.

These competing demands on young people increase in intensity and frequency as they progress through the educational system, reaching their peak during adolescence. It is interesting to note that this increase parallels declines in the relative scores of American students on international comparative tests of academic performance. Given this array of enticements and pressures to spend time on things other than academic work, it is in some ways surprising that many young people are able to devote as much time and effort as they do to their schoolwork. For most students, however, these competing demands place real limits on the amount they can learn in school.

The very existence of these demands and the way everyone involved in the educational system, from students to parents to teachers, responds to them reflects in part the ambivalence about the importance of academic achievement that pervades American culture. Most parents want their children to "have it all." They want them to excel in school, to be good at a sport, to develop social skills and to be part of a group, to learn how to play a musical instrument, to learn to date members of the opposite sex, and often to get experience holding a job. They also want and expect their children to begin to learn how to make choices for themselves and to manage their own energy and efforts. On top of it all, they want their children to have fun.

Acceptance of the legitimacy of this array of goals for children has, of course, important effects on the schools and the way they operate. Inevitably, schools are complicit in the bargains that enable students to pursue these many goals simultaneously. Time is set aside during the school day for band practice, for athletics, and, indeed, for social activities. Teachers make treaties with students that reduce expectations for academic performance and free up time for other activities in return for order in the classroom. In a variety of ways, schools legitimize differential expectations about the academic performance of different students; some are expected to work hard and do well in school, others are encouraged to spend more time in athletics, or music, or some other activity. These differential expectations and the priorities associated with them produce the results that many parents, as well as students, want from our educational system.

It is difficult to imagine major changes in the priorities our society sets for how young people allocate their energies. Even if it were possible to induce such changes in attitudes, it seems unlikely many parents or their children would be receptive. Few Americans could be persuaded to reduce significantly the emphasis placed on sports in high school, turn off the television set, prevent our young people from attending the school dance, or keep our teenagers from working at the local fast food outlet. The best that can be hoped for is to try to strike a better balance between the emphasis placed on academic achievement and everything else that clamors for students' attention.

It must also be acknowledged, however, that our country has potential to address some of the problems over which our students have no control, but which prevent many students from engaging in learning. These include parental unemployment, inadequate family income, family instability, poor nutrition and health, crime and violence in communities, and inadequate housing. Rothstein argues persuasively, for example, that investments in nonschool institutions such as income supports, housing, and health insurance could have a greater impact on the academic achievement of disadvantaged children than current modest increases in school budgets (Rothstein 2002). He concludes that one should not assume that a focus on school policies is the only or even the best way to increase student achievement because families, communities, and broader social policies all have an important impact.

CONCLUSION

The value that Americans place on academic achievement in school has a direct and powerful affect on the predisposition of our children to become engaged in learning, to work hard, and to stay engaged, even when the learning is difficult. These values also affect the choices that parents and children make about how they will apportion their time and energy among competing demands and opportunities. Finally, the priority Americans attach to academic achievement also is likely to influence indirectly the ability to overcome the first three barriers to engagement in learning: increasing expectations that all students can succeed if they work hard, increasing the rewards available to our students, and eliminating inefficiencies in the learning process.

Is there a way to increase, even modestly, the importance most Americans attach to academic achievement in school? If my analysis of the reasons why so many of students are minimally engaged in learning is correct, even a small shift in the emphasis the nation places on academic achievement could have a very big impact. The opportunity for dramatic improvements in the accomplishments of students and schools is apparent, as are many of the steps that must be taken to realize such a goal.

As a society, Americans have a mixed record of success in attempts to modify the attitudes or behavior of a large proportion of its citizens. Without question, the most successful campaign to change both attitudes and behavior of large numbers of people in recent years has been the effort to get people to stop smoking. At least among major segments of the population, the effectiveness of this campaign over the last twenty-five years has been remarkable. Public information and advertising campaigns have also influenced other public health issues in important ways, ranging from the implementation of seat belt laws for children to greater awareness of the role of nutrition in disease prevention. Some success also has been achieved in raising public awareness of the importance of the environment and in generating support for a variety of environmental issues. On the other hand, less success has been achieved in the war against drug use, in reducing alcohol abuse among teenagers, and in efforts to reduce the amount of violence on television.

The effectiveness of the antismoking campaign, among others, however, demonstrates that it is possible to modify the attitudes and beliefs of a large proportion of the population, including many who weren't sure they wanted their attitudes and behavior changed, through the concerted efforts of many people over time. In this context, a modest increase in the priority attached to academic achievement is possible. The first step toward this goal, however, is recognition that up to now, schools have been delivering to most of Americans exactly what they want them to deliver. Schools cannot be expected to change until Americans confront directly their own values and beliefs about the importance of academic achievement and the engagement of their children in the learning process.

Education's preeminent historian, Lawrence Cremin, once noted that "America's educational malaise is rooted in deeper social conditions that won't disappear simply because the country adopts a set of national standards and assessments. In particular, the U.S. has always been a nation with a strong anti-intellectual bent, and that isn't going to change overnight" (*From Risk to Renewal* 1993, 9). Willingness to place academic achievement higher on personal and collective lists of priorities, therefore, is crucial to improving the performance of schools and young people alike. In urging greater attention to student motivation and engagement in learning, a recent report of a National Research Council Committee on a Strategic Educational Research Program concluded that

> No amount of research and no attempts at reform are likely to strengthen learning unless students themselves are willing to work hard. The challenges of today's world require a level of knowledge and expertise that cannot be acquired without effort, even by the most able students. From the early grades, learners must exert themselves to pay attention, to carry out assignments, to study and review challenging material, and they must somehow be motivated to do these things. (National Research Council 1999a, 29)

Finally, as a society, we must also confront again the fact that the school is only one of the two principal socializing institutions in society, the other being the family. Increasing the engagement of students in learning academic skills is only partly—perhaps not even primarily—the responsibility of the school. Without the active support and participation of the family in producing and sustaining students who are motivated to engage in learning, all of our efforts at school reform seem doomed to fail. As psychologist Robert Evans put it recently,

> If we are serious about leaving no child behind, we must broaden our notion of accountability, accepting that the school's impact is more modest

than we wish, the family's more robust than we have acknowledged. How can we truly imagine any broad, significant, enduring improvement in school outcomes without a corresponding improvement in the family as a "readier" and "sustainer" of students? (Evans 2002)

Accomplishing this goal, in turn, requires ensuring that all families have the resources they need to play their crucial role in preparing and encouraging their children to become engaged in learning. The implications of this fact must be taken into account in the struggle to find the right balance between competing goals for ourselves and our children.

The question that all Americans must ask themselves is: "Do we care?" How high a priority should be placed on academic achievement, as opposed to other goals for our children? For a very important subset of children and their parents, as well as other members of the society, these questions are easily answered. Academic achievement comes first and the result is a group of highly motivated and engaged students, supported by families and communities that are committed to making sure their young people succeed. These students do well in spite of whatever barriers they may encounter in their schools or the society at large.

America's overarching ambivalence about the importance of academic achievement, however, contributes directly to intermittent engagement in learning and mediocre performance, at best, on the part of a majority of students. On a larger scale, this ambivalence also affects in important ways investments in the educational systems: in teacher salaries, in training and professional recognition, in research and development, in facilities and equipment, and in a host of ancillary services and programs. It also influences the willingness to tackle seriously the special problems of the most disadvantaged families and students.

Ironically, it seems clear that increasing the engagement of more students in learning is an achievable goal. The current policy emphasis on creating better measures of academic achievement and holding schools accountable for the performance of their students may turn out to be a useful first step toward this goal. Like so many of the school-reform efforts that have preceded it, however, by itself it does not help to address many of the issues raised in this book, including, most importantly, the question of the priority everyone is prepared to place on the academic accomplishments of future generations of Americans.

REFERENCES

Alderman, M. K. 1999. *Motivation for achievement: Possibilities for teaching and learning.* Mahwah, N.J.: Lawrence Erlbaum.

Bandura, A. 1969. Social learning theory of identificatory processes. In *Handbook of socialization theory and research,* edited by D. A. Goslin. Chicago: Rand McNally.

——. 1977. *Social learning theory.* Englewood Cliffs, N.J.: Prentice Hall.

——. 1986. *Social foundations of thought and action: A social cognitive theory.* Englewood Cliffs, N.J.: Prentice Hall.

——. 1997. *Self-efficacy: The exercise of control.* New York: Freeman.

Barton, P. E. 2001. *Facing the hard facts in education reform.* Princeton, N.J.: Educational Testing Service.

Barton, P. E., R. Coley, and H. Wenglisky. 1998. *Order in the classroom: Violence, discipline, and student achievement.* Princeton, N.J.: Educational Testing Service.

Baumrind, D. 1971. Current patterns of parental authority. *Developmental Psychology Monograph* 4, no. 1 (part 2): 1–103.

Blum, R. W., C. A. McNeely, and P. M. Rinehart. 2002. *Improving the odds: The untapped power of schools to improve the health of teens.* Minneapolis: Center for Adolescent Health and Development, University of Minnesota.

Brim, O. G. 1969. *American beliefs and attitudes about intelligence.* New York: Russell Sage.

Bronfenbrenner, U. 1970. *Two worlds of childhood: Childrearing in the U.S. and USSR.* New York: Russell Sage.

Brophy, J. 1981. Teacher praise: A functional analysis. *Review of Educational Research* 51, 5–32.

Brown, B. B. 1993. School culture, social politics, and the academic motivation of U.S. students. In *Motivating students to learn: Overcoming barriers to high achievement,* edited by T. M. Tomlinson, 63–98. Berkeley, Calif.: McCutchan.

Carter, L. S., L. A. Weithorn, and R. E. Behrman. 1999. Domestic violence and children: Analysis and recommendations. *The Future of Children* 9, no. 3 (Winter 1999).

Child Trends. 2001. *Facts at a Glance* (August). Washington, D.C.: Child Trends.

Child Trends. 2003. *American teens*: A special look at "what works" in adolescent development in partnership with the John S. and James L. Knight Foundation Washington, D.C.: Child Trends.

Clasen, D. R., and B. B. Brown. 1985. The multidimensionality of peer pressure in adolescence. *Journal of Youth and Adolescence* 14: 451–68.

Coleman, J. S. 1961. *The adolescent society.* New York: Free Press.

College Board. 2002. *College-bound high school seniors, 1961–2001,* tables and related items. New York: College Board.

Covington, M. 1992. *Making the grade: A self-worth perspective on motivation and school reform.* Cambridge: Cambridge University Press.

Cremin, L. 1961. *The transformation of the school: Progressivism in American education, 1875–1957.* New York: Random House.

Csikszentmihalyi, M., and R. Larson. 1984. *Being adolescent: Conflict and growth in the teenage years.* New York: Basic Books.

Dweck, C. 2000. *Self-theories: Their role in motivation, personality, and development.* Philadelphia, Penn.: Psychology Press.

Education Week. 2002. *Quality counts 2002: Building blocks for success.* Washington, D.C.: Editorial Projects in Education.

Evans, R. 2002. Family matters. *Education Week* 21, no. 37 (May 22).

Everhart, R. 1983. *Reading, writing, and resistance: Adolescence and labor in a junior high school.* Boston, Mass.: Routledge.

Finkelstein, B. 1989. *Governing the young: Teacher behavior in popular primary schools in nineteenth-century United States.* New York: Falmer Press.

Forum on Child and Family Statistics. 1999. *America's children: Key national indicators of well-being.* Washington D.C.: The Forum.

From risk to renewal: Charting a course for reform. 1993. Washington, D.C.: Editorial Projects in Education.

Gardner, H. 1991. *The unschooled mind: How children think and how schools should teach.* New York: Basic Books.

Gewirtz, J. L. 1969. Mechanisms of social learning: Some roles of stimulation and behavior in early human development. In *Handbook of socialization theory and research*, edited by D. A. Goslin, 57–212. Chicago, Ill.: Rand McNally.

Goslin, D. A. 1963. *The search for ability: Standardized testing in social perspective.* New York: Russell Sage.

———. 1967. *Teachers and testing.* New York: Russell Sage.

Graham, S. 1984. Communicating sympathy and anger to black and white students: The cognitive attributional consequences of affective cues. *Journal of Personality and Social Psychology* 47: 40–54.

Graham, S., A. Taylor, and C. Hudley. 1998. Exploring achievement values among ethnic minority early adolescents. *Journal of Educational Psychology* 90: 606–20.

Graham, S., and B. Weiner. 1993. Attributional applications in the classroom. In *Motivating students to learn: Overcoming barriers to high achievement*, edited by T. M. Tomlinson, 179–96. Berkeley, Calif.: McCutchan.

Graubard, S. R. 1995. Preface to the Daedalus issue "American education: Still separate, still unequal." Proceedings of the American Academy of Arts and Sciences, vol. 124, no. 4. Cambridge, Mass.: American Academy of Arts and Sciences.

Hampel, R. L. 1993. Historical perspectives on academic work: The origins of learning. In *Motivating students to learn: Overcoming barriers to high achievement*, edited by T. M. Tomlinson, 21–40. Berkeley, Calif.: McCutchan.

Herman, R., et al. 1999. *An educator's guide to schoolwide reform.* Arlington, Va.: Education Research Service.

Hoff, D. J. 2001. U.S. students rank among the world's best and worst readers. *Education Week* 21, no. 15 (December 12): 7.

Holton, G., and D. Goroff. 1995. Where is American education going? Report of a convocation. *Daedalus* 124, no. 4: 1–42.

Howard, J. 1995. You can't get there from here: The need for a new logic in education reform. *Daedalus* 124, no. 4: 85–92.

Index of Leading Cultural Indicators. 2001. *Empower.org* at www.empower.org/execsumm.pdf (accessed January 20, 2003).

James, W. 1890. *The principles of psychology.* Vol. 2. New York: Henry Holt.

Johnston, L. D., P. M. O'Malley, and J. G. Bachman. 2001. *Monitoring the future survey: National results on adolescent drug use.* Bethesda, Md.: National Institute on Drug Abuse, National Institutes of Health, U.S. Department of Health and Human Services.

Kerrebrock, N., and E. M. Lewit. 1999. Child indicators: Children in self-care. *The Future of Children* 9, no. 2 (Fall).

Kozol, J. 1991. *Savage inequalities: Children in America's schools.* New York: Crown.

Larner, M. B., R. E. Behrman, M. Young, and K. Reich. 2001. Caring for infants and toddlers: Analysis and recommendations. *The Future of Children* 11, no. 1 (Spring/Summer).

Marks, H. M. 2000. Student engagement in instructional activity: Patterns in elementary, middle and high school years. *American Educational Research Journal* 37, no. 1: 153–84.

Maslow, A. 1954. *Motivation and personality.* New York: Harper.

McCaslin, M., and T. L. Good. 1993. Classroom management and motivated student learning. In *Motivating students to learn: Overcoming barriers to high achievement*, edited by T. M. Tomlinson, 245–61. Berkeley, Calif.: McCutchan.

McDougal, W. 1926. *An introduction to social psychology.* Rev. ed. Boston, Mass.: John W. Luce.

McLaughlin, M. W., and L. A. Shepard. 1995. *Improving education through standards-based reform.* Stanford, Calif.: National Academy of Education.

McNeely, C. A., J. M. Nonnemaker, and R. W. Blum. 2002. Promoting student connectedness to school: Evidence from the National Longitudinal Study of Adolescent Health. *Journal of School Health* 72, no. 4.

Miller, N. E., and J. Dollard. 1941. *Social learning and imitation.* New Haven, Conn.: Yale University Press.

Moore, O. K., and A. R. Anderson. 1969. Some principles for the design of clarifying educational environments. In *Handbook of socialization theory and research*, edited by D. A. Goslin. Chicago, Ill.: Rand McNally.

Mosteller, F., R. Light, and J. Sachs. 1996. Sustained inquiry in education: Lessons from skill grouping and class size. *Harvard Educational Review* 66: 797–842.

National Association of Secondary School Principals (NASSP). 1996. *The mood of American youth.* Reston, Va.: NASSP

National Center for Education Statistics. 1996a. *National Household Education Survey 1996.* Washington, D.C.: National Center for Education Statistics.

National Center for Education Statistics. 1996b. *Youth Indicator 41: Sports participation: Percent of population seven years old and over participating in sports activities in the past year, by age: 1986 to 1994.* Washington, D.C.: National Center for Education Statistics.

National Center for Education Statistics. 1996c. *Youth Indicator 42: Employment status of sixteen- and seventeen-year-old students enrolled in school: 1970 to 1993.* Washington, D.C.: National Center for Education Statistics.

National Center for Education Statistics. 1999. *Highlights from TIMMS:*

Overview and key findings across grade levels. Washington, D.C.: National Center for Education Statistics.

National Center for Education Statistics. 2000. *Dropout rates in the United States: 1999.* Washington, D.C.: National Center for Education Statistics.

National Center on Education and the Economy. 1996. *New standards: Student performance standards.* Washington, D.C.: National Center on Education and the Economy.

National Commission on Excellence in Education. 1983. *A nation at risk: The imperative for educational reform.* Washington, D.C.: U.S. Government Printing Office.

National Education Commission on Time and Learning. 1994. *Prisoners of time.* Washington, D.C.: U.S. Government Printing Office.

National Research Council. 1985. *Mathematics, science, and technology education: A research agenda.* Washington, D.C.: National Academy Press.

National Research Council. 1999. Committee on Developments in the Science of Learning, edited by J. D. Bransford, A. L. Brown, and R. R. Cocking. *How people learn: Brain, mind, experience and school.* Washington, D.C.: National Academy Press.

National Research Council. 1999a. Committee on a Feasibility Study for a Strategic Education Research Program. *Improving student learning: A strategic plan for education research and its utilization.* Washington, D.C.: National Academy Press.

National Research Council. 1999b. Committee on Learning Research and Educational Practice, edited by M. S. Donovan, J. D. Bransford, and J. W. Pellegrino. Washington, D.C.: National Academy Press.

National Research Council. 2003. Committee on Increasing High School Students' Engagement and Motivation to Learn. *Engaging schools: Fostering high school students' motivation to learn.* Washington, D.C.: National Academy Press.

Nelson-LeGall, S. 1993. Perceiving and displaying effort in achievement settings. In *Motivating students to learn: Overcoming barriers to high achievement,* edited by T. M. Tomlinson, 225–44. Berkeley, Calif.: McCutchan.

———. 1998. Help seeking, achievement motivation, and the social practice of intelligence in school. In *Strategic help seeking: Implications for learning and teaching,* edited by S. A. Karabenick. Mahwah, N.J.: Lawrence Erlbaum.

Newmann, F. M., G. G. Wehlage, and S. D. Lamborn. 1992. The significance and sources of student engagement. In *Student engagement and achievement in American secondary schools,* edited by F. M. Newmann, 11–39. New York: Teachers College Press.

Nicholls, J., and A. Miller. 1984. Development and its discontents: The differentiation of the concept of ability. In *Advances in motivation and achievement*, vol. 3: The development of achievement motivation, edited by J. Nicholls. Greenwich, Conn.: JAI Press.

Ogbu, J. 1992. Understanding cultural diversity and learning. *Educational Researcher* 21: 5–14.

———. 1997. Understanding the school performance of urban blacks: Some essential background knowledge. In *Children and youth: Interdisciplinary perspectives*, edited by H. Walberg, R. Reyes, and R. Weissberg. Thousand Oaks, Calif.: Sage.

Organization for Economic Cooperation and Development (OECD). 2000. *Knowledge and skills for life: First results from the OECD programme for international student assessment (PISA) 2000*. Paris: OECD.

Osofsky, J. 1999. The impact of violence on children. *The Future of Children* 9, no. 3 (Winter).

Parsons, J., C. Kaczala, and J. Meece. 1982. Socialization of achievement attitudes and beliefs. *Child Development* 53: 322–39.

Peak, L. 1993. Academic effort in international perspective. In *Motivating students to learn: Overcoming barriers to high achievement*, edited by T. M. Tomlinson, 41–62. Berkeley, Calif.: McCutchan.

Phillips, D., and G. Adams. 2001. Childcare and our youngest children. *The Future of Children* 11, no. 1 (Spring/Summer).

Piaget, J. 1962. *Play, dreams, and imitation*. New York: Norton.

Pintrich, P. R. 2000. An achievement goal theory perspective on issues in motivation terminology, theory, and research. *Contemporary Educational Psychology* 25: 92–104.

Pintrich, P. R., and D. H. Schunk. 1996. *Motivation in education: Theory, research, and applications*. Englewood Cliffs, N.J.: Prentice Hall.

Powell, A., F. Farrar, and D. Cohen. 1985. *The shopping mall high school*. Boston, Mass.: Houghton Mifflin.

Public Agenda. 1997. *Getting by: What American teenagers really think about their schools*. New York: Public Agenda.

Resnick, L. 1995. From aptitude to effort: A new foundation for our schools. *Daedalus* 124, no. 4: 55–62.

Rosenthal, T. L., and B. J. Zimmerman. 1978. *Social learning and cognition*. New York: Academic Press.

Rotberg, I. 1991. Myths in international comparisons of science and mathematics achievement. *The Bridge* (Fall): 3–10.

Rothstein, R. 2002. Out of balance: Our understanding of how schools affect society and how society affects schools. Paper prepared for the thirtieth anniversary conference of the Spencer Foundation. January, Chicago, Ill.

Ryan, R. M., and E. L. Deci. 2000. Intrinsic and extrinsic motivations: Classic definitions and new directions. *Contemporary Educational Psychology* 25: 54–67.

Schunk, D. H. 1987. Peer models and children's behavioral change. *Review of Educational Research* 57: 149–74.

Shanker, A. 1995. Education reform: What's not being said. *Daedalus* 124, no. 4: 47–54.

Shiono, P. H., and L. S. Quinn. 1994. Epidemiology of divorce. *The Future of Children* 4, no. 1 (Spring/Summer).

Simon, H. A. 1996. Observations on the sciences of science learning. Paper prepared for the Committee on Developments in the Science of Learning for the Sciences of Science Learning: An Interdisciplinary Discussion. National Research Council, National Academy of Sciences.

Skinner, B. F. 1953. *Science and human behavior.* New York: Free Press.

———. 1968. *The technology of teaching.* New York: Appleton-Century-Crofts.

Skinner, E., and M. Belmont. 1993. Motivation in the classroom: Reciprocal effects of teacher behavior and student engagement across the school year. *Journal of Educational Psychology* 85: 571–81.

Starfield, B. 1997. Health indicators for preadolescent school-age children. In *Indicators of children's well-being,* edited by R. M. Hauser, B. V. Brown, and W. R. Prosser, 95–111. New York: Russell Sage.

Steinberg, L., B. Brown, and S. Dornbusch. 1996. *Beyond the classroom: Why school reform has failed and what parents need to do.* New York: Simon and Schuster.

Stevenson, H. W., and J. W. Stigler. 1992. *The learning gap: Why our schools are failing and what we can learn from Japanese and Chinese Education.* New York: Simon and Schuster.

Stigler, J. W., and J. Hiebert. 1999. The teaching gap: Best ideas from the world's teachers for improving education in the classroom. New York: Free Press.

Stipek, D. 2002. *Motivation to learn: Integrating theory and practice.* Boston, Mass.: Allyn and Bacon.

Surber, C. 1984. The development of achievement-related judgment processes. In *Advances in motivation and achievement,* vol. 3: The development of achievement motivation, edited by John Nicholls. Greenwich, Conn.: JAI Press.

Tanner, D. 1993. A nation truly at risk. *Phi Delta Kappan* (December): 288–97.

Thelen, M. H., R. A. Fry, P. A. Fehrenback, and N. M. Frautschi. 1979. Therapeutic video-tape and film modeling: A review. *Psychological Bulletin* 86: 701–20.

Thomas, J. W. 1993. Expectations and effort: Course demands, students' study practices, and academic achievement. In *Motivating students to learn: Overcoming barriers to high achievement*, edited by T. M. Tomlinson, 139–78. Berkeley, Calif.: McCutchan.

Tomlinson, T. M. 1993. Education reform: The ups and downs of good intentions. In *Motivating students to learn: Overcoming barriers to high achievement*, edited by T. M. Tomlinson, 3–20. Berkeley, Calif.: McCutchan.

U.S. Department of Education, National Center for Education Statistics. 2001. *The condition of education 2001*. NCES 2001-072, Washington, D.C.: U.S. Government Printing Office.

U.S. Department of Education, National Center for Education Statistics. 2002. *The condition of education 2002*. NCES 2002-025, Washington, D.C.: U.S. Government Printing Office.

U.S. Department of Health and Human Services, National Institute for Child Health and Human Development. 2000. *Teaching children to read: An evidence-based assessment of the scientific research literature on reading and its implications for reading instruction*. NIH Pub. no 00-4769. Washington, D.C.: U.S. Government Printing Office.

U. S. Department of Labor. 1991. *What work requires of schools: A SCANS report for America 2000*. Washington, D.C.: U.S. Government Printing Office.

Viadero, D. 1998. On the wrong track? *Education Week* 18, no. 7: 27.

Wagner, T. 2002. *Making the grade: Reinventing America's schools*. New York: Routledge Falmer.

Webb, F. R., M. V. Covington, and J. W. Guthrie. 1993. Carrots and sticks: Can school policy influence student motivation? In *Motivating students to learn: Overcoming barriers to high achievement*, edited by T. M. Tomlinson. Berkeley, Calif.: McCutchan.

Weinstein, R. S. 1993. Children's knowledge of differential treatment in schools: Implications for motivation. In *Motivating students to learning: Overcoming barriers to high achievement*, edited by T. M. Tomlinson, 197–224. Berkeley, Calif.: McCutchan.

Wellman, H. M. 1990. *The child's theory of mind*. Cambridge, Mass.: MIT Press.

Wentzel, K. R. 2000. What is it that I'm trying to achieve? Classroom goals from a content perspective. *Contemporary Educational Psychology* 25: 105–15.

———. 2002. The contribution of social goal setting to children's school adjustment. In *Development of achievement motivation*, edited by A. Wigfield and J. Eccles. San Diego, Calif.: Academic Press.

White, R.W. 1959. Motivation reconsidered. *Psychological Review* 66: 297–333.

White, S. 2002. Personal communication.

Wigfield, A., and J. Eccles. 1994. Children's competence beliefs, achievement values, and general self-esteem: Change across elementary and middle school. *Journal of Early Adolescence* 14: 107–37.

———. 2001. The development of competence beliefs, expectancies for success, and achievement values from childhood through adolescence. In *Development of achievement motivation*, edited by A. Wigfield and J. Eccles. San Diego, Calif.: Academic Press.

Wood, G. H. 1992. *Schools that work*. New York: Penguin Books.

Youth Risk Behavior Survey. 1999. U.S. Department of Health and Human Services, Centers for Disease Control.

Zimmerman, B. J. 2000. Self-efficacy: An essential motive to learn. *Contemporary Educational Psychology* 25: 82–91.

Zimmerman, B. J., and D. H. Schunk, eds. 2001. *Self-regulated learning and academic achievement: Theoretical perspectives*. Mahwah, N.J.: Lawrence Erlbaum.

INDEX

autonomy, need for, 60
autotelic folk models, 64

B
Barton, Paul, 131, 136
bell curve of intelligence, 166
Bill and Melinda Gates Foundation, 109, 171
Binet, Alfred, 35
Bronfenbrenner, Urie, 133–134
Brown, B. B., 148–149
Bruns, Jerome H., 47

C
Central Park East Secondary School, vi, 13n, 94
certification of skills, 168
Clasen, D. R., 148
classroom management, 158–160. *See also* discipline in the classroom
Coleman, James S., 148–149
communally organized schools, 108–109
competence: definition of, in an area of inquiry, 99; need for, 60
competing demands for students' effort, 139–162, 177–179
complexity, and engagement in learning, 67
computers. *See* technology; television and computers
corporal punishment, 159
cost of elementary and secondary education, in the U.S., 119
Cremin, Lawrence, 181
criticisms of schools, 11
crowds. *See* adolescent peer groups
Csikszentmihalyi, Mihaly, 133
cultural influences on engagement. *See* social and cultural influences

curiosity, 18
curriculum: diversity of, 114–117; inefficiencies of, 115–116; uniform, need for, discussion of, 174

D
dating, 150–151
David and Lucile Packard Foundation, 146
Deci, E. L., 60
Dewey, John, 58
discipline in the classroom, 156–160
discovery learning, 93–94
disruptive behavior in the classroom, 158
dissemination of knowledge, to teachers, 174
divorce. *See* family instability
domestic violence, data on, 154
drugs and alcohol, 25; data on use by students, 155
Dweck, Carol, 43–44

E
economies of scale, 115–116
educational agents, 174–175
educational technology. *See* technology
effort:
as an investment, 85–86; based model, 51; competing demands for, 177–179; learning how to use, 110–112; management strategies for, 112; organizing, 85–122; valuing, 123–137; vs. ability, beliefs about as barrier to learning, 166–168; vs. ability, beliefs about the importance of, 26, 33–53, 166–168; waste of, 172
elementary and secondary education, cost of, 119

ABOUT THE AUTHOR

David A. Goslin is past president and CEO of the American Institutes for Research in the Behavioral Sciences (AIR) and former executive director of the National Research Council's Commission on Behavioral and Social Sciences and Education (CBASSE). He is the author or editor of four books, including: *The Search for Ability: Standardized Testing in Social Perspective, Teachers and Testing, The School in Contemporary Society*, and the *Handbook of Socialization Theory*. He received his PhD in sociology from Yale University and his bachelor's degree in psychology from Swarthmore College.